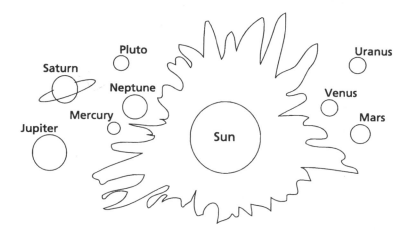

Pluto

Saturn

Uranus

Neptune

Venus

Mercury

Mars

Jupiter

Sun

THE ENLIVENED ROCK POWDERS

Still there are moments when one feels free from one's own identification with human limitations and inadequacies. At such moments, one imagines that one stands on some spot of a small planet, gazing in amazement at the cold yet profoundly moving beauty of the eternal, the unfathomable: life and death flow into one, and there is neither evolution nor destiny; only being.

–Albert Einstein

The Enlivened Rock Powders

by Harvey Lisle

Acres U.S.A.

The Enlivened Rock Powders

Acres U.S.A.
P.O. Box 91299
Austin, Texas 78709 U.S.A.
(512) 892-4400 • fax (512) 892-4448
info@acresusa.com • www.acresusa.com

Printed in the United States of America

Publisher's Cataloging-in-Publication

Lisle, Harvey
The enlivened rock powders / Harvey Lisle. Austin, TX, ACRES U.S.A., 1994
    xiv, 194 pp., 23 cm.
    Includes Index
    Includes Bibliography
    ISBN 978-0-911311-48-8 (trade)

Excerpts from *The Healing Clay* copyright © 1977, 1979 by Swan House Publishing
    Company. Used by premission from Carol Publishing Group.

    1. Minerals in agriculture. 2. Minerals in plant nutrition. 3. Micronutrient
    fertilizers. 4. Sustainable agriculture. 5. Energy in agriculture. I. Lisle,
    Harvey. II. Title.

S587.5.M54 L57 2008   631.8

For Louise

TABLE OF CONTENTS

Foreword . . . . *x*

1. Rudolf Steiner, The Seer 1
2. The Birth of the Planet 15
3. Crystal Power, Rock Power, Living Power, Spiritual Power 29
4. The Silica Rock Powders 37
5. The Lime Rock Powders 49
6. The Clay Rock Powders 57
7. The Zeolite Rock Powders 71
8. Enlivening and Balancing The Soil 77
9. Sustainable Agriculture 87
10. Soil Structure, Drought, Cold, Insect and Disease Resistance 97
11. Enzymes, Vitamins, Minerals and Sunshine 109
12. Bread From Stones 117
13. Ancient Wisdom Transformed 129
14. Radionic Amplification of Paramagnetic Forces . . 149
15. Neutralizing Noxious Forces 155
16. Biodynamic Forces 161
17. Dowsing 169
    Grammar of the Subject 177
    Index 187

"DUST THOU ART"

The "dust" of our cells is the dust of the soil. We should frequently meditate on the words of Ash Wednesday: "Man, remember that you are dust and that you will return to dust." This is not merely a religious and philosophical doctrine but a great scientific truth which should be engraved above the entrance to every Faculty of Medicine throughout the world. We might then better remember that our cells are made up of mineral elements which are to be found at any given moment in the soil of Normandy, Yorkshire or Australia; and if these "dusts" have been wrongly assembled in plant, animal or human cells, the result will be the imperfect functioning of the latter.

–Andre Voisin
   in Soil, Grass and Cancer

ACKNOWLEDGEMENT

As I look back at the panorama of my life I can pick out the individuals who influenced me in the direction whereby I could write this book. I start off with my dad, Clarence Lisle, who insisted that my education must include a major in chemistry. A good working knowledge of chemistry was vital to understanding the many relationships of rock powders. My wife, Louise, loves gardening and was the one who got me into gardening, first organic gardening, and later, Biodynamic gardening. This interest later materialized in making a career of agriculture.

Rudolf Steiner, founder of Biodynamic agriculture, inspired me with his knowledge of the inner workings of agriculture. I decided that this was the ideal path for agriculture to take and I would take it. E.R. Kuck was the founder and president of Brookside Laboratory, New Knoxville, Ohio. He took me into the laboratory where I worked under his wife, Lucille. Together, they gave me the opportunity to pursue my special interests in agriculture.

Clifford Myer and Ike Falb were selling and servicing commercial rock powders to farmers who were their customers. I went with them on many of their travels and had first hand experience with the benefits and pitfalls of rock powders. Dr. William Albrecht was a consultant for Brookside Laboratory, visiting us several times a year. He inspired in me an appreciation of lime and other rock powders. Later on I worked under Dr. Victor Tiedjens who was probably the foremost advocate of liming the soil. Much of his knowledge rubbed off on me.

Charles Walters and his wife, Ann, organized the *Acres U.S.A.* trip to Egypt, followed by the trip to Greece where I picked up on dowsing and much of the information found in this book. Charles Walters suggested that I write this book and gave invaluable help in putting it together. Even as Charles Walters and I share many concepts, we shared in many of the concepts put forward in this book. There were a number of other people I lovingly remember who gave unselfishly of their knowledge which surfaces here and there throughout the book.

FOREWORD

Join with me on a time travel. We will journey back to the days of megalithic man. In his wisdom he built the great pyramids, obelisks, round towers, Stonehenge, stone circles, the Easter Island statues, steles and numerous other megalithic structures. Where did these people get the knowledge and wisdom to build such structures? Were their leaders inspired by the gods? What was the purpose of these structures? Did the stones they used have properties beyond the science of today?

The masons of today trace their beginnings back at least as far as King Solomon's Temple—maybe back to Cheops' pyramid—maybe further back yet. There was a big burst of their activity in the cathedral building era in Europe. It started approximately in A.D. 1000, and lasted for about 300 years before it tapered off. The architects of those cathedrals were inspired men much wiser than we in the value of stones. They knew not only the value of stones but of form, Earth energy lines, sitting locations and sitting directions. For example, they knew the value of spires and their attraction of cosmic forces. The forces these spires pulled into the cathedral flooded the worshipers, aiding the sanctity of the services.

The advent of the Dark Ages marked the loss of this wisdom. The time was soon to come for the birth of science and science would have none of it. Sir Isaac Newton (1642-1727) was undoubtedly more responsible for ushering in the age of science than any other man.

This is the beginning of a new age and the old wisdom will be revived—not necessarily in the form in which it was lost, but as a new form not dependent upon science. We will again turn to stones, form, cosmic and earthly energies. Those of us who work with stone powders will be the spiritual heirs of megalithic man and the early masons who built pyramids and cathedrals. Building a soil may not be as glamorous as building a cathedral but it is essential to healing our Earth and restoring our health.

And so this book is dedicated to restoring some of the knowledge and wisdom held by our ancient forbears.

1

RUDOLF STEINER, THE SEER

Some few eons of time after the Earth cooled, it came to man that there were geysers of creative spirit and active growth in the cosmos, and these explained the growth of garden plants and trees, even the mosses that cling to the mighty oaks in the rainbelt South. Warmth, moisture, air, fertile soil, sprouting seeds, decaying vegetables and certain rock powders—dusts of the soil, as Andre Voisin put it—all preside over the biology of growth more than those icons of modern science known as N, P and K.

Rudolf Steiner pointed out the sources of these forces and how we could actively harness them for plant production. Rudolf Steiner also correctly identified the roles of silica, lime and clay. In a very real sense what he revealed about rock powders is the foundation for this book.

He was standing on the shoulders of giants, of course, starting with the *New Testament* stories of Christ mixing clay with spittle to effect miraculous cures. Modern science either dismisses or confirms, based on its peculiar set of standards, norms, expectations, dogma and rules. And so it has assembled clues based on minerals in silica, or on the presence of aluminum, magnesium, titanium, iron, calcium, potassium, manganese and other elements in earthly compounds, often to be confounded by accomplishments of the substance never envisioned in the components of its makeup.

Indeed, the mysteries become magnified under scientific

scrutiny. Quartz is silicon dioxide. Yet add a minute amount of iron and use more time, behold, the amethyst is born. Adding water accounts for the opal. Sapphires are aluminum oxide married to a little iron. Rubies mean the parent material has given board and room to a fraction of chromium. This may seem as interesting material for a quiz show, no more, until we are faced with the claim that rubies effectively treat high blood pressure, and amethyst guard the lungs and throat from a disease demonology. Or, in a moment of reflection, we are led to the discovery that sapphires assist the circulatory system much as opals relate to the pineal gland.

Clays, crystals, and the grand miscellany known as dusts of the soil, rated consideration long before hunting and gathering gave way to soil tillage. Gilgamesh endured because of this soil magic, and the Greek Dioscorides gave credit to the properties of clay for his extraordinary strength. Pliny the Elder devoted an entire chapter of *Natural History* to the subject. Michael Abehsera, in *The Healing Clay*, tells us that Russian soldiers received 200 grams of a special clay as rations, and the healing arts the world over rely on various mixtures—Cutler's earth in France, for instance—because "duplicating its properties through chemical or physical means is impossible." Life plus life equals life. Dead plus dead equals dead. Mere chemistry cannot rebuild life. Indeed, there is a secret life in the enlivened dusts of the earth, and Rudolf Steiner made it his business to bring this reality into a modern context.

Who was Rudolf Steiner and what was the overriding mission of his life? He was born in Austria in 1861, where he received a good education at both the high school and college levels. During his school years he trained for a career as a teacher of mathematics, chemistry and the natural sciences. Although he never became a school teacher, his education served him well throughout his life. Early on, he discovered that he was a citizen of two worlds, a material world and a spiritual world. He was equally at home in both. It was his intimacy with the spiritual world which prepared him for his life's work as a "spiritual scientist," if such a term can be permitted. He founded the Anthroposophical Society. As its leader he gave over 6,000 lectures, many of which eventually found their way into books.

Although he was never a gardener or a farmer, Steiner was invited to give a lecture course to the farmers who were in the Anthroposophical Society. The year was 1924, and already the impact of the movement initiated by Justus von Liebig's findings was having dire effects in agriculture. This was exactly thirty years after Julius Hensel published his book, *Bread From Stones*, in which he spelled out the evils of chemical agriculture. Now, Steiner weighed in against the evils which had grown even more severe. There were problems in animal husbandry and the raising of crops which threatened the viability of continued farming. There seemed to be no solutions to the problems. To say that he was invited to give the course is a little mild. He was beseeched to give the course. His health was failing and it proved to be the last year of his life. He died in 1925.

No such course was ever given before and it is highly unlikely that such a course will ever be given again. Steiner examined the spiritual aspect of farming, an aspect which dealt with the whole cosmos. Only a highly spiritualistic person could have brought such a message into the material world.

The course consisted of eight lectures given in as many days at the farm of Count Keyserlingk at Koberwitz, Ger-

The Universe

Recent discoveries in biology, geology, chemistry, physics, and astronomy indicate that the universe is nothing at all like the "Great Machine" Western science assumed it was for the past three hundred years. A growing number of scientists now suggest that the universe is more like an evolving, maturing, organism—a living system—which has been developing for fifteen billion years. It has become increasingly complex and diversified, beginning with hydrogen, then forming galaxies, stars and planets, and evolving more complex life-forms over time. The universe, in us, *as us*, can now consciously reflect on itself, its meaning, what it is, and how it developed. "The human person is the sum total of fifteen billion years of unbroken evolution now thinking about itself," Teilhard de Chardin noted a half century ago.

—Michael Dowd
in a monograph, The Big Picture

many. This was a very large farm lying in the eastern part of Germany, which later experienced the ravages of both World Wars. The course is now known as the *Agricultural Course*, and is available in book form from a few sellers. Since the course was given for the benefit of all mankind, I feel free to extract relevant passages. I will not quote them verbatim because Steiner's language is not easily understood by the uninitiated. But I will try to interpret these passages as clearly as possible. There will arise some questions which can be cleared up only after reading the next chapter.

The first rock powders to be considered are those in which the silicious content is paramount. To quote: "Consider the earthly soil. To begin with, we have those influences that depend upon the farthest distances of the Cosmos—the farthest that come into account for earthly processes. These effects are found in what is commonly called sand and rocks rich in silica. Sand and rocks rich in silica are in reality no less important than any other materials found in the soil. They are most important for unfolding the growth processes and they depend throughout on the influences of the Sun and the far planets, Mars, Jupiter and Saturn. Improbably as it appears at first sight, it is through the sand and silica-rich rocks that there comes into the Earth what we may call ethereal life and the chemically influential elements of the soil. These influences then take effect as they ray upward from the Earth through the plants."

The way the soil grows inwardly alive and develops its own chemical processes depends above all on the composition of the sandy portion of the soil. What the plant roots experience in the soil depends in no small measure on the extent to which the cosmic life and cosmic chemistry are seized and held by means of sand

and silica rich rocks, which may well be at a considerable depth beneath the surface of the soil. Therefore, whenever we are studying plant growth, we should be clear as to the geological foundation out of which it arises. For those plants in which the root nature is important, we should never forget that a silicious soil, even if it be only present in the depths below, is indispensable. I would say, thanks be to God that silica is very widespread on Earth. It constitutes 27% to 28% of the surface of the Earth and for the quantities we need, we can reckon practically everywhere on the presence of silica.

Then Steiner goes to clay. Although he doesn't say much about clay, it will be dealt with in depth later on in another chapter of this treatment. "All that is connected by means of silica with the root, nature must also be able to be led upwards through the plant. It must flow upward. There must be constant interaction between what is drawn in from the Cosmos by the silica, and what takes place in the aerial parts of the plant. The roots are supplied by the Cosmos, but they must also be in mutual interaction with what is going on in the aerial parts. In a word, that which pours down from the Cosmos and is caught up beneath the surface must be able to pour up again. And for this purpose is the clay in the soil. Everything in the nature of clay is in reality a means of transport, for the influences of cosmic forces within the soil, to carry them up from below.

"When we pass onto practical matters, this knowledge will give us the necessary indications as to how we must deal with a clay soil, or with a silicious soil, according as we have to plant it with one form of vegetation or another. First, we must know what is really happening—that clay is the carrier of the cosmic upward stream. Secondly, we must know how to treat a clay soil to make it fertile."

Then Steiner goes on to lime. "But this upstreaming of the

cosmic influences is not all. There is another process which I may call the terrestrial or earthly and which depends upon a type of external *digestion*. For plant growth, in effect, all that goes on through summer and winter in the aerial parts of the plant is essentially a type of *digestion*. All that is thus taking place through a type of digestion, must, in its turn, be drawn downward into the soil. Thus, a true mutual interaction will arise with all the forces and fine homeopathic substances which are engendered by the water and air above the Earth. All of this is drawn down into the soil by the greater or lesser lime content of the soil. The lime content of the soil itself, and the distribution of lime substances in homeopathic dilution immediately above the soil—all of this is there to carry into the soil the immediate terrestrial forces."

We thus see that Steiner defines three distinct types of rock powders, each with its own cosmic background and each with its own effect upon crops. These three types of rock powders, silica, clay and lime will be dealt with respectively in their own chapters later in this book.

As we progress with my outline, we will discover that some of the rock powders have forces and some do not. While this treatise is essentially about rock powders with forces, there are other materials with forces which Steiner describes in *Biodynamic Agriculture*. For those who are interested in forces other than those found in rock powders, a chapter on Biodynamic Agriculture will be included later on.

The riddle of the rocks could have been unraveled only by a person with perceptive spiritual insight. Rudolf Steiner was that person. It was my good fortune to have been given the opportunity to work with rock powders for many years and eventually to see the connection between what Rudolf

Steiner told us and our present agriculture. This story will now lead us through some of my own early experiences working with rock powders.

It was approximately thirty years ago when I was an analytical chemist at Brookside Research Laboratories, New Knoxville, Ohio, that I started working with farmers and some small companies which supplied farmers. Besides working in the laboratory as a chemist, I also had a small clientele of organic farmers and their suppliers with whom I worked as a consultant on my own time. Ike Falb was the sales manager for the Anvil Mineral Products Company, based in Bay Springs, Mississippi, where they had their mine. They sold Micro-Min as a soil amendment. Also, they had several animal feed supplements. You will note that most companies which deal in rock powders use them both for soil amendments and animal feed supplements. This could be one tip-off that these rock powders do indeed have life. Anvil's rock powder was a marcasite clay rich in both iron and sulfur.

At the same time I was doing some work for Cliff Myer who was the sales manager for Planters Soil Conditioner. Their rock powder was rich in calcium, sulfur and silica. It was quarried in Colorado near Salida. To the best of my knowledge, these were the first rock powders sold commercially for agricultural purposes, and I was fortunate to be in on the ground floor of both of them. These rock powders did a good job when used correctly and under proper conditions. We knew that they worked, but we didn't know why they worked. Planters also was used both as a soil amendment and an animal feed supplement.

Subsequently, these two companies went out of business. They were pioneers in their movement, bucking powerful adversaries and the inertia of chemical agriculture. It is a

LET ROCKS THEIR SILENCE BREAK

"Your acid clay is nothing more than one that doesn't have the positive ions on it—hydrogen, calcium, potassium, magnesium, sodium and the trace elements. I've got to have 65% of that clay's capacity loaded with calcium, 15% with magnesium. I've got to have four times as much calcium as magnesium. You see why we ought to lime the soil? We ought to lime it to get it up to where it feeds the plant calcium, not to fight acidity." That was Dr. William Albrecht speaking into an *Acres U.S.A.* tape recorder. The formal paper giving expression to these findings was given at the International Society of Soil Science the day Hitler moved into Poland, 1939. It was a technical paper in which Albrecht summarized the work of about a dozen graduate students. What Albrecht was saying seems transparently obvious now. First, agronomists knew little about the real nature of fertility. Second, they knew little about the inventory of land nature had bestowed. In one Missouri county, 16% of the farmsteads had been abandoned between 1916 and 1938. In another area surveyed, 40% had been abandoned. In still another study it was revealed that 51,500 acres of Ozark land were being plowed and cropped, although not more than 17,200 acres were suitable for cropping. At the First National Conference on Land Classification, October 10-12, 1940, Albrecht hinted at the direction in-depth research was taking him and his associates. Many of the details were to find expression in *The Development of Loessial Soils in Central United States as It Reflects Differences in Climate*, 1942. Basically, it was found that soils differed widely as they developed from different rock minerals under variable annual rainfall conditions. This pattern changed as one moved west from the humid mid-continent to the arid regions beyond the 95th meridian, west longitude. Annual rainfall at Alamosa, Colorado, 32.5 degrees north latitude, 105 degrees west longitude, was low enough to be but 20% of the annual evaporation from free water surface. Albrecht often used Transeau's precipitation-evaporation map to illustrate the point. Constant ratios of precipitation to evaporation (as percentages) plotted as isobars to represent effective rainfall properly mapped the varied degrees of *constructive* or *destructive* soil development. These isobars delineated the ecologies of crops, livestock, land in farms, efficiency of radio reception, and defective health via problems in nutrition. Hundreds of the Albrecht papers deal with some or all of these observations. *Soil Fertility and Biotic Geography* as printed in *The Geographical Review*, 1957, is concise and excellent. *Nutrition via Soil Fertility According to the Climatic Pattern*, presented in Australia in 1949, is detailed and worth study. *Declining Soil Fertility, Its National and International Implications*, presented to the Fourth Annual Convention, National Agricultural Limestone Association, Inc., 1949, also covers this phase of Albrecht's thinking. But for a matured vision for presentation here, a 1954 refinement seems appropriate. Styled *Let Rocks Their Silence Break*, this paper was read before the Eleventh Annual Meeting of the American Institute of Dental Medicine at Palm Springs, California,1954.

In *Let Rocks Their Silence Break*, Albrecht concluded:

"Perhaps when we give ear more attentively to the voice of the soil reporting the ecological array of the different life forms (microbes, plants, animals, and man) over the earth, we shall recognize the soil fertility—according to the rocks and resulting soil in their climatic settings—playing the major role through food quality rather than quantity, surpluses, prices, etc., in determining those respective arrays. Man still refuses to see himself under control by the soil. Then when we take national inventory of the reserves of fertility in the rocks and minerals mobilized so slowly into agricultural production in contrast to the speed of exploitation of virgin and remaining soil fertility, perhaps thrift and conservatism with reference to the mineral resources of our soils will be the first and foremost feature of our agricultural policy. By that policy we shall build the best national defense, if there is any basis for contending that if wars must come, food will win them and write the peace. May rocks their silence break and speak nationally through a better knowledge of soil for food as the basis of national health and thereby a national strength for the prevention of war and for the simplest road to peace. Our future national strength must rest in our soils."

> —*Charles Walters,*
> *editor of* The Albrecht Papers, *Volume I.*
> *Quotes as indicated.*

rough world out there for organic farmers and their suppliers. But like the Phoenix, they have risen again under the imprimatur of new companies. The marcasite clay quarried at Bay Springs, Mississippi is now sold as Flora-Stim. The silica rock powder quarried in Colorado is again available.

So let me tell you several stories about these rock powders. Ike Falb had many customers in Lancaster County, Pennsylvania, mostly among the Amish and Mennonite dairy farmers. Lancaster County at that time was the richest agricultural county in the U.S. The main crop was alfalfa, and a devastating thing was happening to it. The alfalfa weevil was dining on alfalfa the way a rich man dines on caviar. This thing was happening to some of Ike's farmers, but not to all of them. There were a few who were raising beautiful alfalfa with only a smattering of weevil damage. Why were the weevils attacking only some of the farms, but not all of them? Ike asked me to go to Lancaster County to try to learn the answer. One of my diagnostic tools is the paper chromatogram which, among other things, reveals soil structure. The chromatograms revealed that where the weevil was present in large numbers, those fields had poor soil structure. All of the farmers investigated were using Micro-Min, so Micro-Min was not the answer. The culprit—which could come as no surprise—was muriate of potash. Farmers who were using Micro-Min and no potash had excellent soil structure and very few weevils. On these farms we could take a three-eighths inch steel rod about three feet long and shove it by hand into the soil nearly to the hilt. No hardpan or plowsole intervened. In the chapter on clays, I will deal with this outstanding property of paramagnetic clays and its propensity to reduce hardpans and plowsoles. We could see the results, but we didn't know how the results came about.

Cliff Myer of Planters Soil Conditioner had a microbiologist, Bob Fram, working for him. Bob and I worked closely together, each of us running our own tests. Invariably, where Planters Soil Conditioner had been used, the microlife increased dramatically. Concurrently, with the increase in microlife would come an increase in organic matter and an improvement of soil structure. Bob, in his tests, would report an increase in microlife. I, in my tests, would report an increase in organic matter and soil structure. Cause and effect remained question marks!

The entire organic movement has the answer backwards. They would say the Planters feeds the microlife and the increased microlife increases the organic matter and the increased organic matter improves the soil structure. This is wrong. It is not the way it works at all. The organic movement has its nose in the soil. Steiner says to set eyes on the stars. Let's go to Steiner and listen to what he has to say.

> Just as we draw in the whole Earth to understand the properties of the compass, so, when we come to the living plants, we must not merely look at the plant or animal or human world; we must summon all the Universe into our counsels! Life always proceeds from the entire Universe—not only out of what the Earth provides. Nature is a great totality; forces are working everywhere. He alone can understand nature who has an open sense for the manifest working of her forces.
>
> What does science do nowadays? It takes a little plate and lays a preparation on it, carefully separates it off and peers into it, shutting off on every side whatever might be working into it. We call it a microscope. It is the very opposite of what we should do to gain a relationship to the wide spaces. No longer content to shut ourselves off in a room, we shut ourselves off in this microscope from all the glory of the world. Nothing must remain but what we focus in our field of vision.

By and by it has come to this: scientists always have recourse, more or less, to their microscope. We, however, must find our way out again into the macrocosm. Then we shall once more begin to understand Nature—and other things too."

Getting back to Planters, bacteria, organic matter and soil structure, Planters brings into the soil living forces from the cosmos. Living forces from the cosmic contribute to increased organic matter and improved soil structure. Bacteria profit from improved conditions, but they do not construct these improved conditions, pulling themselves up by their own bootstraps, so to speak.

Let's go back to Lancaster County, Pennsylvania, to those farmers who found to their dismay that Micro-Min was a loss if they had used muriate of potash. Agricultural chemicals are water soluble and fall under the category of electrolytes. An electrolyte is any substance which in solution is dissociated into ions and is thus capable of conducting an electric current. We should think of soil as a giant condenser with both positive and negative energies, but these energies must be insulated one from the other. If these energies are insulated from each other, the crops can use them in their growth. If the soil has had chemicals (electrolytes) such as muriate of potash applied, these energies are shorted out and the Micro-Min has gone for naught.

The bottom line for those who are using rock powders or expect to use rock powders, *don't use chemicals*. The two are incompatible. The chemicals will render the rock powders useless.

2

THE BIRTH OF THE PLANET

How does the effectiveness of rock powders relate to the birth of the Earth? Certainly, dusts of the soil are part of the Earth. Even as the Earth came into being, so did rock powders. What affects the parent Earth also affects the rock powders.

When was our Earth born and what was its early history? It will be of little value to go to the scientists for this answer because they simply do not have the answer. They theorize on the birth of the solar system from a material standpoint, perhaps with their own subjectivity in tow, forgetting that *subjective* means "a product of the mind unrelated to reality." They point to the vast inventory of cosmic dust, rock particles and asteroids in the solar system. They theorize on the accretion of these material masses into our Sun and planets. Scientists do not deal with the spiritual. They deal with only those things which can be measured and proved in terms of the measuring system they have adopted. Yet the birth of our solar system and of our Earth has its genesis in the spiritual realm. Our story teller is Rudolf Steiner, and we can read his words as the allegory of a clairvoyant, the insight of a metaphysicist, or a vision of science to be. The story is very complex and he goes into quite some detail. I will abbreviate his narrative to tell the story in the idiom we all understand. To do this, it will be necessary to relate the three stages of matter to the fourth stage, which is the spiritual stage.

We are all aware of the solid, liquid and gaseous stages of matter, but beyond these is the spiritual stage, or imponderable matter. The spiritual stage is a *warmth* stage. We think of warm soil, warm water and warm air, but in these instances the word *warm* is an adjective. What we want is pure warmth unattached to any physical matter, and we have a good example. How about a "warm heart?" The person with a warm heart has a spiritual quality which cannot be measured by science. This will give us an idea of the type of warmth we are going to deal with. It is not matter. It cannot be measured. It can be felt, but only in a very subtle manner.

The next step we must take is to understand that although the universe of stars looks very chaotic, in actual fact it is very ordered. Each star or star system has its own space in the universe, and it cannot encroach upon its neighbors. There is a high spiritual entity that oversees this system and maintains order. Another step we must take is to recognize that there are high spiritual entities whose workings we are going to follow. The whole system has been carefully planned and executed by these high spiritual entities, and we are going to have to believe in them. Science cannot follow us in this adventure.

An allotted space in the universe has been reserved for us. In this space there is warmth—in a word, spiritual warmth. This space occupies a sphere roughly with its center at the Sun and its outermost boundary somewhat beyond Saturn. Only you must realize that neither the Sun nor Saturn has been born yet. They are only creative ideas in the minds of the creators. We will disregard Neptune, Uranus and Pluto. Although they have attached themselves to our solar system, they were not in it at the beginning. One could say that they are stepchildren.

E=MC^2

E=MC^2, said Albert Einstein, and with that equation he told us how the law of relativity governs the reconversion, preservation and conservation of mass and energy. Energy cannot be destroyed or put out of existence. This comes terribly close to saying everything always was and always will be, much like a Baltimore catechism. Or perhaps it entertains the thoughts set down by Rudolf Steiner in this chapter.

This science view seems inevitable now that matter has lost its central role in the scheme of things. Indeed, scientific investigation no longer has the experimental facilities required to unravel "God."

The Superconducting Supercollider was envisioned as the ultimate test of how it all happened. The idea was to build a 53 mile oval tunnel near Dallas, Texas. Thousands of superconducting magnets were to guide two beams of electrically charged protons in opposite directions a few million times around the ring, the protons being accelerated to an energy level some 20 times larger than ever managed by existing particle accelerators. The protons would then collide hundreds of millions of times each second. Large detectors—some weighing in at tens of thousands of tons—were to record the collisions. The results would tell science how God did it. The cost was being estimated at $8 billion when the project died. It probably would have cost twice as much. Likely as not we would have learned what we already know, that almost all of our energy comes from the Sun, and that....

Two or more protons make an electron.

Two or more electrons make an atom.

Two or more elements make a compound.

Two or more compounds make a substance.

Two or more substances make a cell.

Two or more cells make an organ.

Two or more organs make a system.

Two or more systems make up bodies, human, animal or plant.

Although Steiner puts no time on the birth of our solar system, science now steps in and estimates that this event took place about 4.6 billion years ago. For us, that is when time and space began. At that time, this huge mass of pure warmth started cooling and condensing in size. It condensed down to a gas, the first stage of physical matter. *There are spiritual entities who want their own planet, and they get it,* says Steiner. *The planet, Saturn, separates off from the mainstream.*

We will forget the main stream for a moment and concentrate on Saturn. To start with, Saturn is only gas with no liquids or solids. Over eons of time this gas further condensed down to its present stage, making it smaller than the original Saturn. Now, as we look at Saturn, it has both liquid and solid, but its density is much less than any of the other planets, being only 0.7 that of water. Saturn, in Steiner's cosmology, is the home of many spiritual entities, so that we cannot say there is no life on Saturn. There is life on Saturn, only we will never see it. Saturn is the first born of our solar system. It is the oldest child in the family. It will be related to all of the subsequent planets as the oldest child is to its younger sibling.

The next planet to be born was Jupiter. More eons of time have now elapsed. Further condensations of gas and moisture have occurred. The density has now increased from the 0.7 found on Saturn to the 1.3 found on Jupiter. There are spiritual entities who want to get off the main stream of evolution and form their own planet. This they are permitted to do, so a huge cloud of gas, moisture and a little solid matter separates off. This is Jupiter, a planet so large, 1,400 Earths could fit into its cubed space. Surprisingly, the chemical composition of Jupiter is similar to that of the Sun. Yet Jupiter never caught fire like the Sun. Jupiter has sixteen moons, four of which are large enough to see with a good pair of binoculars. Another principle to bear in mind is that the evolution of our solar system goes hand in hand with the spiritual entities which inhabit it. Every planet, every Moon and the Sun has its own spiritual entities which have not only chosen the celestial body on which to live, but have had a hand in its evolution. And that principle holds good for our Earth and for ourselves. Getting back to Jupiter's sixteen moons means that there were sixteen diverse groups of spiritual entities on Jupiter that either wanted off Jupiter or had to get off. Each group left taking a small portion of their mother planet and forming their own Moon.

The next planet to be born was Mars. More eons of time have elapsed and further condensations of gas, moisture and solids have occurred. The density has now increased from the 1.3 found on Jupiter to the 3.9 found on Mars. Another group of spiritual entities wants to get off the main stream, and they are given permission to do so. They take some of the matter found in the main stream, separate it off from the main stream and form their own planet, Mars. Mars has many gorges and river beds, so Mars at one time had a warmer climate. The average temperature now found on Mars is approximately 50°C. It is postulated that the water on Mars is now contained in the frozen ice caps.

And now we arrive at the Sun, the pivotal point of our solar system. To give you an idea of its size, the giant planet, Jupiter, has a diameter of 142,800 kilometers. The diameter of the Sun is 1,400,000 kilometers or ten times that of Jupiter, whereas the diameter of the Earth is a little dinky 12,756 kilometers. Much of the scientific information for this chapter comes from the January 1985, issue of *The National Geographic*. They present the scientific data quoted here, but leave unstated the density of the Sun. In fact, scientists do not know the density of the Sun, or perhaps instrumentation delivers results they cannot believe. So we will go to Rudolf Steiner for the answer. He says the scientists would be greatly surprised if they could go to the Sun. They would find it a space vacuum, or anti-matter. To put it succinctly, we just don't understand the Sun.

This brings up another cosmic principle. The physical laws which operate on Earth do not necessarily govern the same way on other cosmic bodies. Some physical laws which apply on Earth do not apply on the Sun. The Sun and the planetary bodies, of which the Earth is one, are of opposite polarities. This is the chief principle we see manifested in many of the rock powders. For example, some rock powders are paramagnetic. Other rock powders are diamagnetic. It is the reason why a rudimentary understanding of the origin of our Earth is vital to any understanding of the rock powders.

The mainstream of our solar system has now arrived at the Sun. Matter is still of the conventional type, but now to the gas, moisture and solids a new element is added—light! The light at first is quite feeble, but the physical warmth is coming on. There are some very high spiritual entities afloat—if we can use that term—and the Sun will be their home. But there are many spiritual entities who will not be able to live on the Sun, and they must move on. So, first, the Earth and its spiritual entities move out from the Sun. We are followed by Venus and then Mercury. Now, the Sun is ready to blaze in all of its glory, lighting up our solar system. We are out there in space with our own planet, the Earth.

So now we are at the end of the line, and we have chosen our own planet on which to live. The density of our Earth is 5.5, that of Venus is 5.3 and that of Mercury is 5.4. The closeness of the densities of Earth, Venus and Mercury tells us that we all left the Sun about the same time when the solid matter was getting relatively high. You will recall that the density of Mars was 3.9, so there was considerable condensation of gas, liquids and solids after Mars separated. We have no way of knowing what the density of the Sun might have been when the Earth left the Sun, but sometime between the separation of Mars from the mainstream and our separation from the Sun, more condensation took place. As condensation takes place, the size of a planet decreases. Earth, Venus and Mercury are smaller now than when they left the Sun.

There isn't too much left to tell about Venus and Mercury. They have their spiritual entities even as the Earth has its own. We have a good idea of the spiritual which chose the Earth. They are known as the human kingdom, the animal kingdom, the plant kingdom and spiritual beings involved with the guidance and development of the Earth and its destiny.

I have refrained from dwelling on the mineral kingdom. The mineral kingdom is the common denominator for all of the planets. It, in a certain sense, ties all of the planets together. The mineral kingdom is the basis for our use of the rock powders.

There is one last celestial body which is vitally important to us on Earth, and that is our Moon. The evolution of the Earth was hindered by certain spiritual entities, so they were compelled to leave. Upon leaving they took with them enough celestial material to establish their physical home, the Moon. For those who have difficulty in understanding how the different planets and moons could separate from each other, it should be noted that the planets and moons in the early evolution of the solar system were not solid as we know them today. They were more gaseous and fluid. The

DUST THOU ART

Science, often at war with religion and the mere mention of a spiritual connection, frequently cancels out its authority by exhibiting a child-like understanding of the *Bible*. Either arrogance or ignorance figures in this failure to comprehend the allegories, parables, fables and enigmas dealing with biochemistry, physiology, anatomy, and "astrological operations of man's physical, spiritual body." These words are extracted and quoted from *Healing Through Ionization and the Equations of Life*, by World Ionization Institute, which holds that the *Bible* can be read as a book of nuclear physics crafted to "purposefully, carefully, fearfully" conceal "so those who did not yet comprehend the awesome and astonishing God-power that lies within the atom would not destroy themselves." Here are a few interpretations of the mysteries the *Bible* has revealed, all stated in terms of Carey Reams Biological Theory of Ionization.

Genesis 1:3. "And God said, let there be light!" And there was light transmitted by an undulatory vibrational movement at a velocity of 186,282 miles per second. Light is the first principle of existence. Every macrocosmic and microcosmic atom in existence, regardless of form, is governed by the immutable universal law, "Let there be light."

Ecclesiastes 3:14 . "And I recognize that whosoever the Lord made, it shall be forever; for nothing can ever be added to it and nothing can ever be taken from it. Thus the Lord has so made everything that men should reverence him."

Indeed, why has God made everything from the atom? In the

language of physics, *I, the atom, am composed of particles; the main constituents being protons, antiprotons, neutrons, antineutrons, electrons, and antielectrons. These particles are arranged in a very specific manner in every atom. The protons, antiprotons, neutrons and antineutrons are held together tightly like a bunch of grapes in the middle of the atom. This middle is called the nucleus. The nucleus is the focal point, like the seed of a fruit, or kernel of a nut. It is the essence of origination, the central mass that is gathered in the middle of every atom.*

Corinthians 3:19 . "For the wisdom of the world is foolishness before God. For it is written (*Job 5:13*), He will catch the wise in their own ruses [their deception and tricks] and the design [and counsel] of the crafty will be routed [and exposed]."

Here is an illustration of a phase in an atom's existence. The carbon 666 atom consists of six protons and six neutrons in the nucleus and six electrons which orbit the nucleus throughout the first three inertia energy levels. Because the carbon 666 atom has only three active electron inertia levels, it is always subject to the carbon 666 subatomic transitional death. The planet Earth and all life are made of carbon 666 atoms. This is why everything in the third dimension is subject to sickness, death and decomposition.

Revelation 13:18. "Here is wisdom: He who has understanding, let him decipher the code number of the beast, for it is the same number of man; and his number is 666." Now re-read that quotation with bracketed words that are implied or denote an explanation of the preceding word or statement.

Revelation 13:18 ."Here is wisdom [the cosmic God consciousness from the universal mind]: He who has understanding [the knowledge of the atom], let him decipher the code number of the beast, for it is the same number of man; and his number is 666.

The beast referred to is the uncontrolled power of the carbon 666 atom. When a carbon 666 atom deviates from its process of nuclear evolution, the awesome omnipotent power of the atom is so ferocious that in due time it devours and grinds itself into an infintesimal dust. From dust thou came and into the dust of carbon 666 atoms thou shalt return! Because man is comprised of carbon 666 atoms, he is always subject to being consumed by the hissing cosmic serpent, the beast, and hence subject to death.

Surely the *Bible*—more than a Superconducting Supercollider—holds a key to dusts of life Andre Voisin wrote about.

solids in them were in a soupy stage or a solid-liquid phase. The actual mechanics of the separations are not known for certain. The planets could have flown off from centrifugal force even as drops of water will fly off of a rapidly revolving wheel. The mechanics of the separations is not really that important to us. The separations did occur and that is what counts.

Are we speaking as allegory, or as some C.S. Lewis, writing stories for minds not yet tuned in on the spiritual reality of life? Each will have to answer that question in his or her heart, much as would a growing child after reading the Lewis sextet of Narina tales—*Prince Caspian, The Last Battle,* etc. Science, after all, is merely a statistical study of phenomena. "We try to link facts together by means of laws, that is to say, by qualitative and sometimes quantitative relations," wrote Lecomte dü Noüy in *Human Destiny.* "But these phenomena only exist as such in our brains."

After fifteen billion years we have come to the end of our story on the birth of the Earth. It has really been a story of the birth of our solar system and it really isn't the end of the story in any case. Our solar system should be around for a few billion more years, but I don't know about mankind. In telling this story I feel much like an historian. In the first place, the historian does not know all of the details of the period under consideration. Even with the details he does have, he can't achieve the vantage point more years can bestow. He glosses over other details so that the history he relates takes on a subjective approach to past events. Therefore, those who study history can get only a rough overview and appreciation of past periods. So it is with this rough overview of the history of our solar system.

In putting this story together I could not help but note that both Mars and Venus have had water systems in the past. Mars is now a frozen planet at approximately 50°C with its water frozen at the poles and Venus is baking hot at approximately 470°C with its water boiled away. Our planet is the only one left with a viable water system. What are we going to do about it? The Earth is the gem of the solar system and it is our responsibility to keep it that way. God won't do it for us anymore.

So, let's get back to rock powders. What has all of this history of our solar system to do with rock powders? What are the common denominators of our planets? It can't be humans or animals or plants as they are found only on Earth. Rocks are found on all of the planets. From a study of meteorites, it has been established that the rocks on one planet are similar to the rocks on the other planets. They all have a common origin and are quite similar. Another common denominator is our Sun. Our Sun is the same Sun for all of the planets in our solar system.

Rudolf Steiner, in his *Agricultural Lectures*, referred again and again to the "near planets" and the "far planets," so let's find out how he differentiated them.

Near Planets	*Distance from the Sun*
	(kilometers)
Mercury	57,900,000
Venus	108,200,000
Earth	149,600,000
Far Planets	
Mars	227,900,000
Jupiter	778,300,000
Saturn	1,427,000,000

The Sun has two different warmths. I have described its spiritual warmth, a warmth with which we are not familiar.

It also has a material warmth with which we are very familiar. We are all familiar with warm sunny days. The spiritual warmth as manifested in silica comes from the Sun, but is modified by the "far planets" Mars, Jupiter and Saturn. The material warmth as manifested in lime comes from the Sun, but is modified by the "near planets" Mercury, Venus and the Moon. As far as the Earth is concerned, the Moon is rated as a planet.

We have traveled a long route to understand why lime and silica are polarities. Silica brings us the forces from "far planets" Mars, Jupiter and Saturn as channeled through the spiritual warmth of the Sun. Lime brings us the forces of the "near planets" as channeled through the material warmth of the Sun. Our rocks pick up these forces. As we learn to work with our rocks we learn to work with the other members of our solar system.

3

CRYSTAL POWER, ROCK POWER, LIVING POWER, SPIRITUAL POWER

Let us explore a silica crystal and find out what mysterious powers it holds. We will first consider the mundane energies that can be measured by current scientific methods such as electricity, light, heat and mechanical means. After that we will consider the cosmic energies found in celestial bodies. We make this division, artificial though it may be, for a very important reason. We can describe quite precisely the behavior of the mundane energies within crystals, and from these descriptions we see that there are certain parallels with the spiritual energies contained also.

The forces which bind a crystal together are in perfect balance and harmony. Therefore it can be said that crystal is in a perfect state of equilibrium. Crystals are taking in and giving off energy constantly, and they are doing so in perfect balance. The amount of energy given off is exactly equal to the amount of energy taken in, consequently the crystal itself remains unchanged.

The first behavior we will examine is the piezo-electric effect. Strike the crystal with a mallet compressing the structure momentarily. There will be a flash of visible light and a burst of electricity. This effect takes place only when the crystal is struck and electrons are released. After the momentary discharge of electrons the crystal will rapidly replace the electrons from the air.

This process can be reversed by sending electricity into the crystal. There will be an alternative expansion and contraction resulting in a subtle vibration. This process is utilized in an electronic watch and in some pressure gauges.

As a boy, I made a crystal radio set which seemed like pure magic. It still seems like pure magic after all these years. A silica crystal was utilized to tune in a local radio station. There wasn't enough power to energize a speaker, for which reason I had to use earphones. There was a "feeler" which had to touch the crystal on a precise point. This evidently vibrated the crystal in resonance with the frequency of the radio station. Now I was tuned in and could listen to the program.

Another behavior we can explore is known as pyroelectricity. As the crystal is heated, electrons are discharged, creating an electric current. Upon cooling, the crystal replaces the lost electrons with others collected from the air.

We can't leave out computers. The heart of the computer is the silicon chip or crystal. When computers started getting popular, I had to make the decision whether I would get into them or stick with what I knew the best. I opted to stick with what I knew best, but I can tell a good story about them. I have a younger brother who has gotten into computers. He also loves to work with genealogy. In fact he has worked up our family genealogy to where by pushing several keys he can bring onto the screen almost any information about our forebears you could ask for. He can probably do the same for anyone's genealogy, based on data previously inserted into the system. Give him a few basic keys about a family, he will go to one of the fine genealogy

A Philosophical Connection

If use of enlivened rock powders depends on a spiritual connection, it also is explained by a countervailing view away from materialism, agnosticism and the social Darwinism that once swept the field. These extremes first were answered in the writings of Henri Bergson and Pierre Teilhard de Chardin.

Bergson was born in 1859, the year *Origin of Species* came on-scene. He studied Herbert Spencer, but rejected materialism. He saw the evolutionary process as a sort of mechanical elimination of the unfit, albeit in terms of *élan vital*, or a surge of life. As a philosopher he discovered the laws of nature and nature's God well beyond Democritis' atoms or Galileo's space-time to make a spiritual connection. His work was called *Creative Evolution*, meaning "true evolutionism and consequently the true continuation of science."

These ideas motivated Teilhard de Chardin, a scholastic. As a young man, during World War I, he received the Military Medal and Legion of Honor for bravery above and beyond the call of duty. Later he became a Catholic priest and a paleontologist. He spent his life "under suspicion of heresy" by his Order and condemnation for his teleological ideas by scientific colleagues. Because he had vowed obedience, publication of his work, *The Phenomenon of Man*, awaited his death in 1955. These were timely developments, for the god called science had already failed. It simply ran into questions for which scientific testing had no answers.

libraries in the United States via a computer network, and in only a few minutes he will tell you many things about your genealogy you never knew. Computers are both science and spiritual science. Some of the best scientific minds in our country are involved in developing the capabilities of the computer *ad infinitum*. But ever at the heart of the computer is the silicon crystal. When you get into the crystal, you are getting into spiritual science, and we aren't very good at that yet. In a certain sense, spiritual science is what not only this chapter, but what *The Enlivened Rock Powders* is all about. We are trying to understand why some things happen the way they do. There is something deep inside crystals and rocks which relates to our entire universe. We are trying to get a little understanding of this subject. As we work at it, we are working as spiritual scientists.

From the few examples so far provided, it can be seen that when energy is put into a crystal it will come out, albeit in a different form. Crystals are transformers of energy.

We are now ready to go to the subject of *life*. What is *life*? There are a number of definitions. The one I like best is *self-awareness*. Any entity which is aware of itself has life. A story might best demonstrate life and self-awareness. The story has for its setting a hot day on the farm. You and I are working on this farm making hay and stacking the hay bales on a wagon. After a while we have to quit because of heat exhaustion. We go to an air-conditioned house and pull out of the refrigerator several bottles of ice cold beer with which to refresh ourselves. On this farm there is a pig. Since on that day it got pretty hot, the animal headed for a mud puddle. On this farm there is a patch of sweet corn. The leaves start to wilt in order to cut down on their exposure to the hot sun. There is a large granite stone lying next to the garden and it also gets hot, but there isn't anything the stone can do about it, so we say the stone is dead. In the cases cited above, every life form had self-awareness and tried to do something to alleviate the heat, except the stone. The stone didn't know it was hot and even if it had realized this, there was nothing it could have done to alleviate the heat. That is our mode of thinking simply because we are material people living in a material world, and our thinking is material. What happens if we transform ourselves into spiritual people living in a spiritual world and spiritualize our thinking? The silica in that granite stone is resonating in tune with the silica found in the far planets, Mars, Jupiter and Saturn, and is brought to Earth by that hot Sun. That granite stone has the power to transform some of the cosmic energy it is receiving, and passes it along to the sweet corn. The sweet corn, which has been under stress, is now nourished with cosmic energy and the stress is relieved.

I don't think anyone dares to say that our solar system is dead. Granite stone is part of a living system, albeit a spiritual living system. Don't tell that sweet corn which was perked up by the subtle energy from the stone that the granite dust is dead. If you do, the sweet corn might tell you that you have rocks in your head.

I am not going to go so far as to say the stone is living, but I am going to say the stone is enlivened. It is more than a dead stone. There are rock powders that will pass on the subtle energies received from cosmic bodies. These are living, or enlivened, if you will. Then there are stones or rock powders which are unable to pass on these subtle energies. These, I suppose, could be called lead. This is a book about living or enlivened rock powders. Lest there be any confusion, the granite stone in our story about the sweet corn patch was an enlivened stone. To make sure you have plenty of enlivened stone or rock powders in your garden soil to relieve the stress in your sweet corn, you spread a rock powder such as basalt or any of the other fine commercial rock powders available to growers.

To conform with the materialistic world, I will on occasion use the terms *paramagnetic* and *diamagnetic*, because they imply a polarity in our enlivened rock powders. Polarity is very much a property of rock powders, and we should realize that early on. To quote the discoverer and lead researcher of these properties, Phil Callahan, "Paramagnetism is the ability of a substance to collect or resonate to the magnetic fields of the Cosmos. It is not magnetism." To which I agree wholeheartedly. We are all familiar with the generic use of *man* to mean both men and women. So it is with the term *paramagnetism*. Depending on how the term is used, it could mean one of the polaric properties, or designate a generic term covering both paramagnetism and diamagnetism. Unlike the paramagnetic antennas of insects, which respond to subtle energies, rock powders utilize crystals or crystal-like forms to collect subtle cosmic energies, transforming them into uses from which we can benefit.

There are enlivened powders which do not have their origin in the rocks of the Earth, still they are closely tied to stones. Diatomaceous earth is the best known one. It has its origin in diatoms that lived thousands of years ago in the sea. Diatomaceous earth is not living, but it traces its origin to life. Therefore it properly could be referred to as enlivened. In its long history, it got mixed up with other sea sediments, if you please, so I don't think we would be amiss to call diatomaceous earth a rock powder. Another similar material is marl. There are many marls, including some popular ones on the market.

Look at your fingernails and your hair. Are they living?

ON A PIECE OF CHALK

Long before James Watson and Francis Crick unveiled for science the DNA and RNA of the evolutionary process, debate over the age of the planet Earth was spirited, even intense. On one occasion, Thomas Henry Huxley—"Darwin's bulldog" he was called—faced a group of workers at Norwich, England. The title of his talk was, *On a Piece of Chalk.*

Huxley told those working men how a chalk layer, hundreds of feet deep, ran not only under much of England, but under Europe as well—all the way to the levant in northeast Africa and central Asia. The piece of chalk Huxley spoke about was calcium carbonate. Examination under the microscope revealed it to consist of fossil shells left by life forms in ancient seabeds once in command of the area described. Often the calcium carbonate beds contained fossils of large animals such as crocodiles, often species quite different from those identified with those areas today. Indeed, deep levels of chalk meant changed fingerprints, so to speak, illustrating how the environment changed during the millions of years it took those chalk beds to form.

In Huxley's day, some few "Bible Scholars" invoked childish notions of what scripture really said to prove the Earth was no more than 6,000 years old.

Those millions of little corpses that once drifted down to ancient sea beds now rate attention not only as enlivened rock powder, but also as the king of nutrients for farm crop production.

You can cut them off with no pain or sensation, but I would hope you wouldn't say they are dead. They carry the imprint of your being even after they are cut off. One of the things we use in Biodynamic agriculture is cow horns. They aren't dead or we wouldn't use them. They carry certain cosmic imprints which we are after. Diatomaceous earth is rich in silica, which when enlivened is paramagnetic. There are humates rich in silica which are paramagnetic. Clod Buster is a good example.

If you are convinced that enlivened rock powders do have certain spiritual properties, then the effects from spreading them on your land can be further enhanced. Besides being a material person, you are also a spiritual person. You can use some of your spiritual powers to enhance the spiritual properties of your enlivened rock powders.

Having a green thumb is more than a myth. People with a green thumb are using their spiritual powers whether they realize it or not. Rudolf Steiner tells us that our crops should have more than material fertilizers. They should also have some spiritual input. This is a sad aspect of chemical agriculture. The crops get the material fertilizers, but there are no spiritual inputs, meaning that from a spiritual point of view much of our food is dead. Most of the food we eat fails to nourish our spiritual being. This is apparent in the decline of the moral values in our country. Using enlivened rock powders is an excellent way of getting spiritual values into our crops.

For those readers who are interested in this aspect of agriculture, I have added an extra chapter near the end of the book on Biodynamic agriculture, a form of farming vitally concerned with the spiritual as well as the material aspects of food production.

4

THE SILICA ROCK POWDERS

Since it was Rudolf Steiner who called our attention to the importance of silica in agriculture, I think it is appropriate to quote from several of his lectures.

"Turning our attention to the earthly life on a large scale, the first fact for us to take into account is this. The greatest imaginable part is played in this earthly life by all of that which we may call the life of the silicious substance in the world. You will find silicious substance in the beautiful mineral quartz, in the form of a prism. You will find the silicious substance combined with oxygen in the crystals of quartz." He goes on.

Imagine the oxygen removed from quartz and you have the elemental silicon. Silicon is one of our 92 elements. Now we must not forget that the silicon which lives thus in the quartz is spread over the Earth so as to constitute 27% to 28% of our Earth's crust. Silicon is the second most abundant element in the Earth, the most abundant element being oxygen. Thus an enormous quantity of silicon is present. Now it is true this silicon occurring as it does in rocks like quartz appears in such a form that it does not seem very important when we are considering the other material aspect of the Earth with its plant growth.

Quartz is insoluble in water—the water trickles through it. It therefore seems to have very little to do with the ordinary conditions of life. But you need only remember the plant Equisetum, or horsetail, contains 90% silica. From all of this, you can see what an immense significance silicon must have. But the peculiar thing is how very little notice is taken of it. It is practically excluded today even from those domains of life where it could work most beneficially.

Throughout Nature, silicon plays the greatest imaginable part, for it not only exists where we discover it in quartz or other rocks, but in an extremely fine state of distribution it is present in the atmosphere. Indeed, it is everywhere. What does this silicon do? Let us assume that we had only half as much silicon in our earthly environment. In that case our plants would all have more or less pyramidal forms. The flowers would all be stunted. Practically all plants would have the form of cactus, which strikes us as normal. The cereal grasses would look very queer indeed. Their stems would grow thick, even fleshy, as you went downward.

I think it would be helpful to comment upon Steiner's statement that silica is found in a fine state of distribution in the atmosphere. Over the years I have spent considerable time in Florida, where I am always intrigued by the Spanish moss growing in trees. Spanish moss is a bromeliad or an air plant. There are many other bromeliads growing in Florida, but Spanish moss is the most visible one. These plants grow in trees, but they get their nourishment from the air. They use the trees only as a structure on which to grow. After one winter trip to Florida, I brought home a bushel of the Spanish moss and since I was an analytical chemist at Brookside Laboratories, I ran a complete analysis on it. It was high in silica and had all of the other so-called agriculturally important elements in good measure—calcium, magnesium, potassium, sodium, phosphorus, sulfur, iron, copper, zinc and boron.

Since scientists cannot conceive of all these elements being found in the air, they say the bromeliads pick up their elements from the dust and the mist in the air. My work was not very scientific since I pulled my Spanish moss out of

THE FLINT STONES

The word silica derives from the Latin terms silex or silicis, which in English is flint. Flint stones, when impacted or struck, emit sparks that can set tinder on fire. Using the spark of flint stones, man no longer needed to carry the "sacred fire" into the caves. The sparking properties of flint gave mankind more freedom and crucial control over the environment. Flint stones bestowed great progress and prosperity of controlled heat. Much later, with the discovery of wooden matches, flint stones were forgotten—for a long while.

Then a time came when evolving man searched for a perfect cover for ventilation holes in his dwellings that would keep out rain and cold but let in the light. Perhaps accidentally, he discovered that flint, as silicates, made ideal window panes. Yes, the most common silicate, silicon dioxide (SiO_2) delivers the raw material for glass. Again flint provided for a man's well-being and comfort—soon taken for granted.

Silica again came to the rescue in modern times when electricians looked for a suitable semiconductor that would control the flow of electric charges. They discovered that silicon exhibited excellent semiconductive properties. This remarkable capacity of flint revolutionized the electronics industry. North America decided to honor the ancient flint stones by naming a giant electronics district "Silicon Valley." Today, people consider the personal computer to be the invention of the century, having the greatest impact on their lives (and most definitely on mine!). Thanks to the flint stones I can save weeks of work by committing this text to the memory chips of my computer.

There is more. The flawless beauty of quartz, as exemplified by the purple amethyst, is nothing less than silicon. More correctly, it's silica. Silicon is one of the few elements (others are potassium and sodium) that cannot exist in isolation on Earth. Only the interior of the Sun can hold single silicon atoms. On this planet silicon is always joined to other atoms, creating useful compounds like silica crystals. And those siliceous crystals are swinging with the times; they even make modern clocks accurate with their "timely" vibrations.

> —*Klaus Kaufmann* ,
> *from* Silica, the Forgotten Nutrient

trees where it was exposed to the dust and mist of the air. But, fortunately, there were several other researchers who were more careful, and raised their Spanish moss in special chambers to exclude any dust and mist from the air. No problems!

So what is the answer to silica being found in the air, or for that matter, most of the other elements also being found in the air? The answer was touched upon in Chapter 2, *The Birth of the Earth*, in which the so-called fourth state of matter was explained. It really is an energy state. Those of us who are aware of these elements in the atmosphere sometimes refer to them as being there in homeopathic amounts. The bromeliads such as Spanish moss have the ability to condense these elements, in energy form, down to the material state.

Steiner spoke and wrote: "The far planets, Mars, Jupiter and Saturn, work upon the silica beneath the Earth's surface, assisting those influences from the Sun which also work beneath the Earth's surface. All that works below the Earth's surface from Mars, Jupiter, Saturn and the Sun to influence the growth of plants works not directly but in this way. It is first received by the Earth and the Earth then rays it upwards. Thus, the influences that rise upward from the earthly soil for the growth of plants are in reality cosmic influences rayed back from the Earth and working directly in the air and water over the Earth. These relationships determine how the earthly soil, according to its constitution, works upon the growth of plants.

"Modern man knows practically nothing of how the light behaves in the interior of the Earth. He does not know that the silicious, that is, the cosmic stone or rock or sand received the light into the Earth and makes it effective there."

THE BROMELIAD FACTOR

It is axiomatic that plants generally cannot get calcium, potassium and phosphorus from the air. As for minor nutrients, most of them are supplied via the air.

"Why don't plants take more of them from the air," asked Carey Reams, who discovered the Biological Theory of Ionization? Fortunately, he stayed on for an answer. "They're not healthy enough. The sap of a plant is similar to the gastric juice in a human being. There are saps and gastric juices that are weak. The weaker the gastric juice in a human being, the sicker that person becomes. The weaker a sap in a plant, the less minerals it can take in from the air. If you grow good produce, people are less likely to become ill. A major cause of illness is mineral deficiency."

–Reams quotations from an oft repeated lecture.

EMPTY FOODS

The alarming fact is that foods—fruits and vegetables and grains—now being raised on millions of acres of land that no longer contains enough of certain needed materials, are starving us—no matter how much of them we eat.

> —*Charles Norton, M.D.,*
> *as reported by Rex Beach in* Cosmopolitan,
> *June 1936.*

I feel that I should comment here that probably the ultra violet rays of the Sun penetrate into the soil, reacting, so to speak, with the silicious content of the soil. I know that sometimes in digging in my soil, I find a little green moss several inches below the surface of the soil. The fact that it is green tells me that the Sun's rays got to it, but how?

Perhaps Steiner comes to our rescue.

"Precisely with regard to this silicious principle, the Earth gradually loses its power in the course of time. It loses it very slowly, therefore we do not notice it. Nor must you forget that modern man seems unconcerned about the loss of silica. He thinks it insignificant for the growth of plants. In reality, it is of the greatest significance. We need the silica to attract and draw in the cosmic forces. Now in the plant there must arise a clear interaction between the silica and the potassium, not the calcium. By the whole way in which we fertilize the soil, we must enliven it, so that the soil itself will aid in this relationship."

Many farmers and gardeners know that the ideal soil for root crops is sandy. The best potato growing regions are areas favored with sandy soils, Maine, Minnesota and Idaho leading the way, although there are potato acres in every one of the lower forty-eight states. Watermelons seem to resonate to silica.

Quartz is one of the most common minerals in the Earth's crust. As SiO_2, it is an important ingredient of all igneous rocks. Some sandstones are almost 100% quartz. Mica, feldspar, granite, basalt, sandstone, orthoclase are other forms of silica minerals. There are literally scores of variations of these silicate minerals.

One very common silicate mineral is coal. The history of coal is as vague as it is interesting. We have been led to believe that coal is the breakdown product of ancient tropical forests. If a tropical forest was cut down and all of its lumber layered and decomposed under anaerobic conditions, not more than a few millimeters of coal would be formed. Yet, many coal deposits are over 100 feet thick. Thus there has to be another answer to the formation of coal. When the Earth was very young and in a more plastic condition, living processes were more mineral, yet also had some plant characteristics. Trees had not even come into being yet. This mineral-plant material grew with great intensity laying down our coal deposits.

Coal is a mineral-plant material. When I was a boy, most homes were heated with coal furnaces. Every winter morning, as the fire in the furnace was renewed, the ashes had to be shaken down through the grates into the ash pit. Saturday was the day to shovel the ashes for storage out of doors, eventually to be hauled away. Most of those ashes were silica.

A well known proprietary coal product for agricultural use is called NutriCarb. It is a bituminous coal rich in sulfur. I have used NutriCarb both in my garden and in my orchard with good results. I mention this because I want to caution the readers that each coal deposit has its own history and the agricultural results from using coal from the different deposits could vary, perhaps unfavorably.

Although I told a little about diatomaceous earth in the preceding chapter, the subject begs for more exposure than it has so far received. Diatomaceous earth is another ancient deposit laid down by a living process. Diatoms are unicellular algae having silicious cell walls. They live in the sea. As they die they settle to the bottom where they often build up to form immense deposits. There are areas in the western United States which were once ocean floor. These high silica deposits are easily mined to furnish us our diatomaceous

DIATOMACEOUS EARTH

Diatomaceae, sometimes known as Bacillarieae, are the microscopic plants related to the algae whose remains make up diatomaceous earth. These diatoms have existed for geologic ages and are still abundant in both salt and fresh water where they serve as food for living organisms and, after decomposition, for other plants. Fossils of dead diatoms, as well as living diatoms, are too small to be seen individually without high magnification. In a living mass they are easily visible as the brown growth on the surface of stagnant water, mud, rocks, and seaweed and other wet surfaces where light and water have been present long enough for the growth to accumulate.

The diatoms are single-celled plants consisting of two parts which fit together in the same manner as the two halves of a pillbox. The frustules are fashioned in countless shapes, rather similar to the complex beauty of snowflakes. There are some 10,000 varieties of diatoms. Reproduction is frequently by subdivision, and the rate of propagation may be extremely rapid, one frustule becoming a billion diatoms in a thirty-day period under favorable conditions.

In many areas over the world, in regions which at one time or another were under water, are found large deposits formed during the Miocene and Pleistocene ages as diatoms died and settled to ocean or lake bottoms. [It can be seen that this rock powder owes its valued properties to the life process.]

—from "Diatomaceous Earth" by William Q. Hull
Industrial & Engineering Chemistry,
February 1953.

earth products.

There are many of these ancient silica bearing sea deposits. One well known marine deposit is trade named Clod Buster. I mention this to illustrate one of nature's gifts and the basic reasons it works as well as it does. There are no two products alike. Their histories may be similar in some respects, but their overall biographies are as different as some of their effects.

These rock powders have gone through a life process, which has been impressed upon them. They have retained a quality which is of value to the Earth and can be of value to agricultural endeavors. All of them are paramagnetic and all of them can impart paramagnetic properties to our soils.

Let's go back and discuss life again. I know we have already touched upon it, but the subject cries for more attention. If you are interested in rock powders and want to use them in the life processes of your garden or farm, the better you understand them, the more successful you should be. These ancient sea or coal deposits or volcanic powders or animal deposits called lime still retain an element of life. They certainly are not living as we understand life, but they are helpmates to the organism that serve the living Earth.

Our Earth is indeed a living entity and it has its organs much as we have ours. The Earth breathes, it has two circulatory systems much as we do, and it exhibits nerves, and a sensory system to those with the wit to ask the right questions. It has a nutritive system and the other necessary defenses for life. Rudolf Steiner explains all of these systems and thereby bestowed on us the insight required to study our legacy of life from stones.

The Earth is very much a part of our solar system. The Sun and the planets are bound tightly together, held in place by a gravitational string. It is common to say that God rules these life processes, but that is an oversimplification. And that is but one reason why we cannot now nor ever will be able fully to understand God. We can believe in God, but we cannot understand Him. We can believe in life, but we cannot understand it either. These paramagnetic and diamagnetic rock deposits are a part of the life processes of our Earth, and as such contain an element of life even though we may not understand it.

I have now dealt with paramagnetic rock deposits from plant processes on our ancient Earth. In the section to come I will deal with paramagnetic rock deposits that are a consequence of animal processes in our ancient Earth. Still there is one class of paramagnetic rock deposits that comes under neither the plant nor the animal process. That class is made up of igneous rocks—basalt and granite, for instance. This class dwarfs all the others in size. Basalts and granites predate both plant and animal processes. Here, our credulity of life is stretched even thinner. Rudolf Steiner would say the igneous rocks date back to when the Earth was in a very hot, vaporous-fluid-gelatinous state. The life here would have to be a carry-over from the ancient Sun which gave birth to planet Earth. Silica is the material carrier of this life.

We have now traced silica as a Sun element that carried life into the extremely hot early stages on an ancient Earth and into the cooler plant stages. We now know we can take the resulting paramagnetic rock deposits which carry a life factor, and by properly utilizing them we can reintroduce or strengthen the paramagnetic life factors of our soils.

A COAL CONNECTION

The carbon that is in NutriCarb coal has both positive and negative energy fields in equal amounts, making it the perfect purifier. This is the reason why NutriCarb is working so well in the area of purification. A method of testing I have developed allows me to test all coal to determine how much energy the carbon can or will absorb. Many coals exhibit toxicity in varying degrees. This causes them to annihilate microorganisms and not to break down or absorb energy, causing it to be toxic. Coal carbon can test toxic in either negative or positive terms. When this storage capacity is used up and the carbon can hold no more toxins, new carbon must be added or the bacteria will be forced to use the old carbon, thus releasing unwanted toxins. This causes unwanted weeds and grasses to grow and unwanted nutrients to debilitate farm crops. When an energy field in the carbon is filled, and it can hold no more, then this energy becomes part of the water in the ground. Nitrates and herbicides in underground water suggest a carbon structure with its absorbing capacity saturated.

—Leonard Ridzon
in The Carbon Connection

5

THE LIME ROCK POWDERS

We are much more familiar with lime than with silica or clay. Most of us have limed our land at one time or another, but we have never considered adding silica or clay to the soil. Do we really understand all of the implications of lime? Practices observed in the countryside do not make this suggestion. Technically lime is calcium oxide, or calcium carbonate, but in the context of this book the concept of lime will be greatly expanded. There is no word or term to adequately cover the subject. We will continue to use the word *lime*, but please understand that it will be used in a much broader sense than usual.

We will start with Rudolf Steiner's lesson on *"lime."* "We find a substance which must occur everywhere throughout the Earth, albeit it is not so widespread as the silicious element. I mean the chalk or *lime* substances and all that is akin to them—lime, potash and sodium substances. If these were present to a lesser extent, we should have plants with very thin stems—plants, to a large extent with twining stems; they would all become creepers. The flowers would expand, it is true, but they would be useless. They would provide practically no nourishment. Plant life in the form which we see today can thrive only in the equilibrium and with cooperation of the two forces, *lime* and silicious substances."

The lime concept of rock powders also includes rock phosphate, gypsum and some sea formations such as coral and sea shells. The most common phosphate rock is apatite with a formula of $Ca_5(Cl,F)(PO_4)_3$. You can see that there is actually more calcium in rock phosphate than there is phosphorus. Thus rock phosphate, with its high calcium content, falls easily into our *"lime"* classification.

Gypsum is $CaSO_4 \cdot 2H_2O$. Gypsum has equal amounts of calcium and sulfur and with its high calcium content falls within the lime classification. Gypsum is neutral, being neither acid nor alkaline in nature.

Coral and seashells contain large amounts of calcium. They, too, fall under the *"lime"* classification, even though they contain significant amounts of silica. In the discussion of silica rock powders, we found that another sea product, diatomaceous earth, fell into the silicious class, which points out that nature has many secrets we have yet to comprehend.

Under the more classical definition of lime, there are high calcium lime, dolomitic lime, burned lime, hydrated lime, feeding lime, stack lime and perhaps a few others. I recently was introduced to stack lime. Our coal burning power plants emit large amounts of sulfur dioxide into the atmosphere. This product goes on to produce acid rain. Under relatively new environmental laws, power plants must now reduce their sulfur emissions. One way to neutralize sulfur is with lime. The end product is stack lime. I have seen no technical data on this material, but it must be high in sulfur. This could make it somewhat like gypsum, which is calcium sulfate. I have known only one farmer who is using stack lime. He is a hay farmer and is dressing his alfalfa fields with this lime entity, and it seems to be doing a good job.

Steiner has a lot to say about sulfur and it is all good, therefore I am hopeful that stack lime will work out well for farmers. Certainly it will lend a mighty assist to keep the environment clean and be a good product for agriculture as

THE SOIL COMPLEX

"Saturation of the soil complex" is so much Greek to most farmers. If you fill a ten-gallon pail full of sand, the space in the pail is saturated with sand. If limewater is added to the sand, it fills the spaces between the sand grains and the sand is saturated with limewater. If you add organic matter, acid, clay, and silt to the sand until the spaces are filled, you would have the sand saturated with organic matter, clay, and silt. Then we would have something resembling an acid soil. The organic matter and colloidal clay still contain minute cavities which are lined with millions of negative charges, each one holding a hydrogen ion. We have a situation similar to a run-down battery, which is useless. The soil is also useless.

–V.A. Tiedjens,
in More Food from Soil Science

well. Sulfur is a key element in proteins. Since most of our soils are low in sulfur, stack lime well might improve the protein quality of many food crops. It has been my experience that all limes are diamagnetic, which makes them polaric to silica rock powders, which are paramagnetic. It has been another of my findings that the less a lime is processed, the more diamagnetic it remains. Lime which is simply crushed and powdered can be the most diamagnetic of them all.

There are approximately ninety-two elements in the Earth today. Calcium is one of them. Yet, if we go back to the very beginning of our solar system, there was only warmth, and no elements. Somewhere in the scheme of things calcium came into being. Just when and how this happened remains unknown. Probably it happened some time after the Earth separated from the Sun. Even as coal is the primordial precursor to plant life, so are huge lime deposits the primordial precursor of animal life. Steiner theorizes that the animal kingdom in the early days of the Earth was not as we know it today. Rather than to try to explain it further, I suggest this is something we will either have to believe or not, as one chooses.

Next, we are required to consider the potassium and sodium based rock powders. There are only a relatively few of them, since both potassium and sodium based minerals are water soluble and cannot exist where there is substantial rainfall. Chile saltpeter is one of them, $NaNO_3$. It practically never rains in the region of Chile where this mineral is found. It was used extensively many years ago for its nitrogen content, and it is still used today, albeit in much smaller amounts by specialty uses. It is diamagnetic, which puts it into the lime category. The principle ores of potassium mined in the United States are sylvinite and langbeinite, both found at Carlsbad, New Mexico. They lie

LANGBEINITE

It is evident that a natural potash-mineral, like langbeinite, may be effectively and efficiently used as a fertilizer when due consideration is given to the inorganic and the organic soil factors in relation to microbial and plant nutrition. The successful management of the interrelated activities of those three lower strata in the biotic pyramid, *viz.* soil, microbes and plants, calls for full appreciation of the following facts:

1. Higher concentrations of either the more-soluble or the less-soluble fertilizers in limited soil volumes will feed the plant for more efficient use of the applied minerals than when the latter are intimately mixed with more soil.

2. The above practice makes the clay efficient in holding the more-soluble materials for ready exchange and the less-soluble for more complete mobilization.

3. Fragments and granules of nutrient minerals in the soil represent focal points of *sustaining fertility*, and more than mere bits of *starter fertilizers.*

4. Deeper placement is not apt to put inorganic fertilizers beyond the prompt reach by plant roots, according to experiments and observations. This holds only for greater depths, but also for wider spacing as much as 14 inches according as placements are deeper.

5. Placement as deep as below many of our surface soils, or into the upper part of the subsoil, represents efficient use of the fertilizer by the plants. It represents, also, the elimination of microbial competition for it since they burn out much of the

organic matter in their struggle for energy or carbon to balance their use of the more soluble minerals.

6. Nature's maintenance of productive humid soils under her climax crops suggests practices for us, when in their evolution the crops and soils conformed to two major conditions. In the first place, there were reserves of the requisite nutrient elements in the weatherable rock minerals throughout the profile and/or they were regularly added to the surface by inwash or wind. In the second place, the organic matter was contributed most completely in place, both as root remains within, and as crop residues on top of the soil.

7. The above facts and factors demand consideration not only for an economic soil management looking toward fertility maintenance, but also for the most complete soil conservation through which alone we can hope for foods and feeds of nutritional quality supporting all strata in the biotic pyramid by which man at its apex is sustained.

When the use of agricultural limestone as a less-soluble, natural mineral fertilizer, supplying calcium and magnesium, has served for so many years in soil restoration and greater agricultural production by following the above, we have an excellent precedent telling us that a natural potash-mineral, like langbeinite, supplying also magnesium and sulfur, can be similarly used to good agricultural and economic advantages.

–William A. Albrecht
in The Albrecht Papers, Volume 1

from 600 to 2,000 feet below the surface of the Earth. What little rainfall there is at Carlsbad would have no effect on these minerals. A common name for this product is sul-po-mag, with and without capital letters. Depending on analysis, several other names have market identity, one being potassium sulfate.

To eliminate any confusion over my usage of the term *lime*, I sometimes write lime in quotation marks, thus, "lime." I use this device to designate the entire classification of lime, rock phosphate, gypsum, potassium and sodium minerals. When I omit the quotation marks as in *lime,* I am referring to the popular use of the word.

There is a type of digestion going on in the aerial parts of plants which is supported by both the "lime" in the soil and the homeopathic "lime" in the atmosphere. These "digestion" products must be pulled down into the roots by the "lime" forces. The lime which we spread on our land sucks down the plant sap that is synthesized in the leaves. This plant sap travels down the phloem cells into the roots, in turn feeding the roots. It also migrates into the fruit or seeds of the plant.

"Observe those plants in which the 'lime' forces strongly draw the earthly nature downward into the roots," wrote Steiner. "These are the plants whose roots shoot in all directions with many ramifications, such as alfalfa. If we have any feeling or receptivity for these things, we can observe the process most wonderfully in the legumes—in all of those plants which are well known in farming as nitrogen collectors. They indeed have the function of drawing in nitrogen, so as to connect it to the soil around. We may truly say, down there in the Earth something is athirst for nitrogen; something is there which needs it, even as the lung of man needs oxygen. It is the '*lime*' principle. Truly we may say, the *'lime'* in the Earth is dependent on nitrogen inbreathing, even as the human body depends upon the inbreathing of oxygen."

Steiner refers to the processes going on in the atmosphere around the plants as a kind of "digestion." Processes going on in the atmosphere are dependent upon the forces coming from the near planets of Moon, Mercury and Venus, as carried by the Sun. We thus see that there is a very clear relationship between the near planets and the "lime" materials we use in agriculture.

For whatever reasons lime is invoked, we now know it has a cosmic aspect which contributes to its effectiveness. I had the privilege of working with two soil scientists who knew the value of lime and advocated its use, William A. Albrecht and Victor Tiedjens. Albrecht recognized lime as part of the wholistic concept of soils. He made his opinion and findings a matter of record in hundreds of scientific and popular reports, many of which have been codified by *Acres U.S.A.* as *The Albrecht Papers*, volumes 1 through 4. Tiedjens left a classical testament on lime—*More Food from Soil Science.* On the other hand, Tiedjens recognized lime as the most important rock powder necessary to keep soils up to par. As a soil consultant, I have many times recommended nothing more than the spreading of some additional lime on the land. At the time I did not recognize the cosmic connection. If we take into account the many material and cosmic values in "lime," we must concede that "lime" is undoubtedly our number one rock powder.

6

THE CLAY ROCK POWDERS

We have now dealt with silica and lime, but according to Rudolf Steiner there is one more basic rock powder to consider, namely clay. Silica and lime are polarities, whereas clay falls in the middle with similarities to both. It is very much like a husband and wife who are polarities. They have a child who has similarities to both parents.

Clay has a very important property not shared with either silica or lime. It is related to the constellations, whereas silica and lime are related to the Sun. There are some properties of silica and lime which shut down at night because that is when the Sun shuts down from a dark side of the Earth point of view. Clay never shuts down because the constellations never shut down.

There are twelve constellations. In the course of a year the Sun passes by all twelve, from which reason we have discerned our twelve months. As the Sun passes a constellation, it transmits to us influences from that constellation. This is only the tip of the complexity involved. In the course of a month, the Moon also passes by all twelve constellations. As it passes, it transmits the influence of each particular constellation. Taking a month as thirty days and dividing thirty by twelve, we get 2.5 days for each constellation. The Moon is a big reflective surface that mirrors these influences back to us. It is interesting to reflect upon the fact that Moon metal is silver, the best reflective metal there is. Suffice it to say, there is much wisdom in the cosmic order

CLAY'S ATTRACTION

Clay has a negative electrical attraction for particles that are positively charged. In the organism most of the toxic poisons are positively charged. These toxins are irresistibly drawn towards the clay. Moreover, according to an authority on Bentonite (another name for the energetic clay) "clay's particles being shaped like a 'calling card' with the wide surfaces negative and the edges of the card positive, have many times more negative than positive pulling power."

The same authority writes the following: "The very minuteness of the particles of Bentonite gives a large surface area in proportion to the volume used, thus enabling it to pick up many times its weight in positively charged particles." According to Robert T. Martin, B.S., University of Minnesota, Ph.D., Cornell University, and mineralogist at Massachusetts Institute of Technology, one gram of this product has a surface area of 800 square meters. The greater the surface area the greater its power to pick up positively charged particles.

—*Michel Abehsera*
in The Healing Clay

of things, and we can understand only a little of it. Constellation forces do not come to the Earth directly, but are reflected by the Moon and the Sun. Clay picks up these reflected forces emanating from the constellations.

There are three rhythmical metals without which life as we know it could not exist. Iron is one of them. It is the breathing element in the blood of mammals. At one moment it transports oxygen from the lungs to the rest of the body. The next moment it transports carbon dioxide produced in the body to the lungs from which it is exhaled. Magnesium is the rhythmical metal for the plant kingdom. It alternates between day and night in the plant's breathing pattern. Aluminum is the rhythmical metal for the soil, where it is positioned as the central and chief element in clay. Aluminum, of course, is the most abundant metal in the Earth's crust.

There are many types of clays and each type has numerous ramifications. Aluminum is basic to each type. It is found in each type and always assumes the center position in the formula of compounds, such as $CaO \cdot Al_2O_3 \cdot SiO_2$. The first group shown in this formula is always a member of the "lime" group, whereas the last group is always a silicate. Because of the rhythmical element, aluminum, clay becomes a rhythmical rock powder. Clay may be either paramagnetic or diamagnetic. When the Sun is shining, it is paramagnetic. When the Moon is shining it is diamagnetic. Sometimes both the Sun and Moon are shining at the same time, in which case the clay is diamagnetic. Sometimes, neither Sun nor Moon is shining, in which case the clay is not active. For now, it is enough to recall that clay acts as a catchpen for influences passed along by the Sun and the Moon acting as reflectors for the constellations.

This is what Steiner meant when he told us that clay is a

means of transport. Certainly, clay assists silica rock powders in moving plant saps from roots to leaf areas and assisting the "lime" rock powders in moving the saps from the leaf areas back to roots. Since the forces in both the silica and "lime" rock powders are dependent upon the Sun, clay rock powders are the only ones working at night, or when the Moon is shining. More accurately, the Moon does not need to shine. It may be the dark of the Moon, but the Moon is still in the sky reflecting forces from the constellations. Cloudy days or cloudy nights do not compromise transmission of cosmic forces.

Sap flow in trees and plants might be compared to the circulation of blood in animals and human beings. A person who has good blood circulation is not affected by the cold as much as a person with poor circulation. The person with the poor circulation will have cold feet, cold hands and a cold nose in cold weather. So it is with trees and plants. A hard winter won't be hard on a tree with good sap circulation. Sap circulation will be considered again when cold resistance, drought resistance, insect and disease resistance are discussed.

Clay, in the orthodox sense, is the geological breakdown of coarser rock particles into extremely fine particles. For example, medium-sized sand has a diameter of 0.50 to 0.25 mm, or approximately 5,700 particles per gram. A typical clay particle is 0.002 mm in diameter. It takes approximately 90,000,000 particles of clay to make a gram. This extreme fineness of clay is very important to the cation exchange capacity (CEC). Clay particles may have calcium attached to them which can be exchanged by plant roots for hydrogen. The plant gets the calcium and the clay particles get the hydrogen. Later on, lime may be applied to the soil. Then the clay takes on the calcium and gives up the hydrogen.

This trading back and forth by the clay particles is a manifestation of its rhythmical properties.

Taconite is an iron ore mined in the Mesabi Range of Minnesota. The use of taconite in agriculture has some strong supporters, including Ford Dickerson and Donald Anderson, both of Minnesota. They think the value of taconite lies in its magnetism. However, its magnetism is quite low and therefore this cannot be the answer. More properly, paramagnetism, or the ability to resonate to a cosmic force, identifies the value of taconite. It does not have aluminum in its formula, whereas clay does, but it has iron, which is also a rhythmical element. Taconite acts like a paramagnetic clay, and a very good one at that.

Perlite and vermiculite are products highly valued in the making of potting mixtures. Both have the paramagnetic properties of clays, even though they are not clays. Their use goes a long way in preventing "damping-off" in young seedling plants. These paramagnetic clays promote good sap circulation, the certain answer to preventing "damping-off."

Bentonite clay is a mixture of aluminum and magnesium silicate minerals and generally comes from weathered volcanic ash. It is used in toothpaste, soaps, washing compounds, paper fillers, adhesives and has hundreds of industrial uses, but of greatest interest to us is its healing properties.

One proprietary clay is known as Pascalite. This clay was discovered by a trapper, Emile Pascal, in 1930, when he observed that Indian medicine men and wild animals knew about it and used it regularly. Emile first used it on his badly chapped hands, which healed promptly.

FloraStim is a commercially mined clay product. It is quarried in Bay Springs, Mississippi. I have seen corn stalks grown on fields where it has been used. When you cut

PARAMAGNETIC, DIAMAGNETIC

Years ago I discovered that Ireland is composed of two types of limestone. One type is highly paramagnetic and is found in the mountainous rim of Ireland. The other type is highly diamagnetic and is the subsoil limestone bedrock that underlies the entire central agricultural bowl of Ireland. Both look exactly the same to the most practiced eye. That diamagnetic bedrock is, of course, overlaid by a rich top covering of highly paramagnetic volcanic soil which eroded down into the bowl from the volcanic rocks of the rim mountains. Ireland, like the Nile Valley, was perfectly designed by God for efficient agriculture—that is before our high-energy insanity took over to ruin it as in the case of the Nile Valley.

Strangely enough, all of the round towers and tower houses that I measured are made out of the highly paramagnetic limestone, even though they are located in the central bowl miles away from the mountainous limestone. Conversely, all of the cotter houses or old peasant cottages that I measured are made of diamagnetic limestone regardless of where they are located. Logical? Fighting and ruling is a charged up, fast moving game, whereas farmers are more easy going and like to relax in their homes after a long day's work with their paramagnetic soil. Those Celtic peoples most certainly knew about the opposite forces in stone, and probably inherited that knowledge from the ancient Egyptians.

—Philip S. Callahan
in Ancient Mysteries, Modern Visions

through the nodes you see a pearly white texture, which is very rare these days. That goes right back to the excellence of sap circulation promoted by paramagnetic clays.

When I worked as an analytical chemist at Brookside Laboratories, Professor William A. Albrecht visited us at least once or twice a year. As a consequence, we were well versed in his agricultural teachings. He taught his students that rock phosphate was a better answer to phosphorous deficiency than superphosphate, triple superphosphate, or any other chemical form of the nutrient. The most available phosphate rock at that time was a 33% hard rock from Florida. Also coming out of Florida was a 20% soft rock phosphate with colloidal clay attached. We encouraged our clients to buy the 33% rock because they would be getting more phosphorous for their money. The 33% hard rock and the 20% soft rock were selling for practically the same price at the time. Some of our clients claimed they were getting better results with the 20% rock in spite of the lower phosphorus values.

To appreciate this judgment, it is important to know how the phosphate was mined. The 33% hard rock was washed out of its deposits with high pressure hoses. It was transported with water through sluices, then separated from the water, dried and bagged, or shipped in bulk. A large volume of water was involved in this operation, and it ended up in a holding basin along with some very fine particle size phosphate and colloidal clay. Eventually, this material was reclaimed from the holding basin and sold as 20% soft rock phosphate with colloidal clay.

Here are a few facts we did not know at the time. The 33% hard rock phosphate is a paramagnetic material falling under the "lime" classification. The 20% soft rock phosphate with its colloidal clay tag-along material is a paramagnetic clay. Thus, they are two different materials acting under two different cosmic influences. Farmers who were getting better results with the 20% soft rock and colloidal clay were benefitting more from the colloidal clay than from the phosphorous.

Another material popular with some organic farmers is greensand. It is sold as a source of potassium, but it contains no more than 6% of the element, which is very slow to release. It always puzzled me how farmers could benefit from its use. The key to this riddle became self-evident as we expanded our knowledge. In fact, greensand is a paramagnetic rock powder similar to clay even though it is not a clay. The more I work with these rock powders, the more surprises I get.

Another well known rock powder is Azomite, which is a montmorillonite clay. It, too, is highly paramagnetic. Azomite has been used successfully to treat the disease called citrus decline, a condition that results from obstructed sap flow. This attribute of Azomite emphasizes again and again the value of paramagnetic clay rock powders in maintaining a healthy sap flow in trees and corn in particular, and in plants in general.

There are a lot of good paramagnetic rock powders waiting to be discovered. To give an example, Rita and Ralph Engelken of Greeley, Iowa were pioneers in the organic farming movement. Ralph became a victim of persistent lender harassment, and passed from the scene. Rita is carrying on with the help of one of her sons. There are five sand and gravel pits in their area, and Rita wondered in silence if at least one of them might contain some paramagnetic materials. She sent me a sample from each. The sand from one of the pits had good paramagnetic properties and I reported back to her that sand would be a nice help in maintaining farm fertility.

Another example: Tim Heintz, who farms in northern Ohio, has worked hard to develop a rock crusher. He took some material from a local sand and gravel pit to put through his crusher. It turned out to have the properties of a paramagnetic clay. I would expect sand to have the paramagnetism of silica rock powders, but this one didn't turn out that way at all. It read more like a paramagnetic clay.

Siegfried and Uta Lubke of Puerbach, Austria operate a truck garden that is world renowned. They got caught in Chernobyl's radioactive fallout because their farm lies downwind from that atomic facility. When tested for radioactive residues, their garden produce came up negative quite early compared to the others in the area, all of which continued to test positive for cesium. Paramagnetic clays have the power to neutralize radioactivity to a large extent. The Lubke method of gardening includes the use of finely ground rock powders. Evidently, the rock powders they used were paramagnetic clays. Admittedly, this is a simplistic explanation. A flourishing microorganism population surely figured in the breakdown equation. Research will no doubt uncover many of the factors that contributed to the neutralization of radioactivity in the Lubke's farm soil. In addition to rock powders, they also use Biodynamic materials, and these undoubtedly helped. Certainly there are other ways to promote paramagnetism in a soil system other than adding rock powders. A highly paramagnetic soil might accomplish the same effects. But the fact remains that a paramagnetic clay will help absorb radioactivity and neutralize it.

Uta and Siegfried Lubke have a fine microbiological laboratory on the farm. This enables them to follow the

ALBERT CARTER SAVAGE

He came to know that the rock in the soil had something to do with the growth of plants. In the beginning there had been abundance of rock and the soil had been rich, but it had been robbed of its richness and more rock was needed to replenish it. His father gave him a little piece of land. He crushed rock and spread it upon the land. The vegetables that he grew were better than his father's. He had something there but it was not enough.

He saw animals languish and waste away and human beings sicken and die before their time. His father died and his great uncle died.

He asked the doctors why this was so, and they couldn't tell him except that disease had fastened upon them and they had gone the way of all flesh. It was the law of life that found its fulfillment only in death.

Their answers didn't satisfy him. There must be a better reason. There must be a fault somewhere that the doctors hadn't found. It wasn't in the sky. It might be in the ground.

Plant life, he knew, was the product of soil, air, sunshine and water. The air elements were constant and shiftable. The sunshine was changeless. The soil elements were inert and stayed where they were except as they were displaced or washed away. The soil was subject to deterioration by natural agencies and unnatural uses, necessitating restoration of its elements. Restoration had been neglected and there had been deterioration of the plants because of the deficiencies of the soil upon which they fed.

Animals fed upon the plants and human beings fed upon the animals and the plants. Could not the basic deficiencies be in that manner communicated to animals and human beings? Savage was satisfied that they could be and that they were, but he knew that he had to prove it.

For years the man applied himself with consuming fervor to the proving of what he knew to be true. There were countless experiments and tests that, by their progressive revelations, strengthened his faith.

Not until 1942 did he write the testament of his faith, though many knew of his work and numbers had claimed benefits in health and well being from the mineralized foods that he offered without money and without price. The pamphlet that he privately printed he called *Mineralization*.

It was his hope that his work would be like a life line thrown out to a stricken world. On the title page he anxiously asked, "Will It Reach You In Time?"

—*from* Profile, *Albert Carter Savage,*
Acres U.S.A., November 1977

activity of microflora in the soils they farm. They have reported that the use of finely ground rock powders promotes the growth of microflora magnificently. They weren't the first to make this observation. Albert Carter Savage discovered the same phenomenon in his Kentucky garden soils in the 1930s. He was a great believer in the use of rock powders. His fame spread to Ohio where as a young man I heard of his results. He, too, had his laboratory to better follow the progress of the microflora in his soils.

The next worker I met—in spirit at least—was John Hamaker, then of Michigan, and only recently deceased. I journeyed to Michigan one weekend to hear him speak. He is the author of the book, *The Survival of Civilization*. John was very much aware of the influence of rock powders in the promotion of microflora in the soils. In one of the articles he wrote for *Acres U.S.A.*, he coined a term, *orgskin*, as the reactive coating left on a rock particle by the action of the microflora.

A fourth person I now need to mention is Vaclav Petrik, a very fine microbiologist who long ago observed the proliferation of microflora in the soil under the influence of newly introduced rock powders. He has his own commercial laboratory in California, specializing in identifying and propagating compost starters and other microbial workers. All the people mentioned here are pioneers in promoting the relationship of rock powders to the proliferation of the microflora and fauna in soils. Still I have to take my stand with Rudolf Steiner, who in essence said we should look to the cosmic bodies for the true benefits of our rock powders rather than to the microflora and fauna in our soils. Microorganisms benefit from the influences brought into the soils by rock powders. They are the effects, not the cause. Cosmic bodies are the cause. I know ahead of time that this argu-

THE CALCIUM KINGPIN

C.J. Fenzau and Charles Walters, ardent students of William A. Albrecht, and Arden Andersen (referring to Charles Northern, Carey Reams and Albrecht), are emphatic that one should not look on calcium as merely an antidote to acidity, but as the most important mineral for balance. They consider calcium to be the kingpin, determining the proportion of other main minerals. It is true, that in recent years, calcium has acquired more importance and become known in more compounds with special uses, such as calmodulin. It does seem that this mineral exerts an earned dominance.

Herbert H. Koepf refers to Albrecht, when lauding the value of calcium. He observes that "high content slows down leaching and release of nutrients from rocks, favors formation of stable and richer forms of humus...and, if sufficiently high, a good crumbly structure in moderately heavy soils...."

A shrewd 1970 comment by A.T. Semple is made in his book on grassland: "The need for lime may be based on the value of the calcium as a plant nutrient rather than on that for correcting acidity of the soil." He continues: "Many legumes grow in soil with a pH much below 7—provided the soil is well supplied with the required nutrients, and provided other factors, such as moisture and temperature, are favorable. Some legumes, e.g. subterranean clover, will grow on only soils that are acidic or neutral. In the tropics, the use of lime may be harmful to legumes—apart from members of the tribes Trifoliae and Vicieae."

—*Bargyla Rateaver in*
The Organic Method Primer Update, 1993

ment will cause a storm of protest and, in all honesty, I could take sides with both camps. My purpose is not to create controversy, but to point out that the benefits from using rock powders are not confined to the proliferation of the microflora and fauna, but also to the cosmic influences introduced into the soil by rock powders, "dusts of the soil," as Andre Voisin put it.

Clay has been known for centuries. It has been used by many peoples for its healing properties. I feel certain that these healing properties are due to its paramagnetism. We can truly say that paramagnetic clay is an enlivened rock powder deriving its beneficial healing properties from its relationship with cosmic bodies. And the cosmic bodies, much like a cosmic Christ in our midst, carry healing forces which can be transmitted by the proper paramagnetic clays. Paramagnetic clays transport enzymes which promote the healing of burns, rashes, infections and a myriad of skin problems. They can also be used internally for intestinal problems, for which reason I now refer the reader to an excellent book, *The Healing Clay*, by Michel Abehsera.

Needless to say, all clays do not have the powers suggested by this chapter. Paramagnetic clays—the clays that have relationships to the constellations, to the Sun and to the Moon—are part of a living cosmic system.

7

THE ZEOLITE ROCK POWDERS

The zeolite rock powders are paramagnetic in nature. Although they are not clays, they act in a manner similar to the clays. They are practically unknown in U.S. agriculture, but are being used successfully in Japan. Some familiarity with them is long overdue, and they certainly have a place of honor in this book. I confess that my knowledge of zeolites is rather limited, therefore I am relying on promotional material supplied by Geo-Environment Services, Inc. of Austin, Texas. Readers who would like more information on zeolites are encouraged to contact these primary suppliers and/or standard texts on minerology.

Since their discovery by the Swedish mineralogist, Baron Cronstedt, in 1756, over forty naturally occurring zeolite minerals have been identified. The name zeolite means boiling stones. The term is derived from the Greek *Zeo*, meaning to boil, and *Lithos* meaning stone. The composite word refers to a conspicuous loss of water when zeolite minerals are heated.

Natural zeolites were discovered as major constituents of numerous volcanic ash deposits in saline lake deposits of the western United States, and of massive marine deposits in Japan and Italy. Since that time, more than 1,000 deposits have been reported from sedimentary rocks of volcanic origin in more than forty countries. The nature and high purity of the natural deposits have aroused considerable commercial interest in the United States and abroad.

THE ZEOLITE FAMILY

The zeolite family of hydrous silicates "live" in the cavities of basalt. All the members of this family—analcime, chabazite, heulandite, natrolite, stilbite—have the capacity for losing and replacing water content without a change in the crystal structure. The family itself is described here with conserved brevity, leaving further definition for the glossary section of this book. *Dana's Manual of Mineralogy* has this to say about the zeolite family:

"The zeolites form a large family of hydrous silicates which show close similarities in composition and in their associations and mode of occurrence. They are silicates of aluminum with sodium and calcium as the important bases. They average between 3.5 and 5.5 in hardness and between 2.0 and 2.4 in specific gravity. Many of them fuse readily with marked intumescence, hence the name *zeolite*, from two Greek words meaning to *boil* and *stone*."

"All the zeolites are aluminosilicates whose gross compositions some what resemble those of the feldspars, and, like the feldspars, are built about chains made up of 4-fold rings of SiO_4 and AlO_4 tetrahedra. The chains, bound by the interstitial cations, sodium, potassium, calcium, and barium, form an open structure with wide channelways in which water and other molecules may be readily housed. Much of the interest in zeolites derives from the presence of these spacious channels. When a zeolite is heated, the water in the channelways is given off easily and continuously as the temperature rises, leaving the structure intact. This is in sharp contrast to other hydrated compounds, as gypsum, in which the water molecules play a structural role and complete dehydration produces structural collapse. After essentially complete dehydration of a zeolite, the channels may be filled again with water or with ammonia, mercury vapor, iodine vapor, or a variety of substances. This process is selective and depends on the particular zeolite structure and the size of the molecules, and, hence, zeolites are used as molecular sieves. Zeolites have a further useful property that derives from their structure. Water may pass easily through the channelways, and, in the process, ions in solution may be exchanged for ions in the structure."

Zeolites have unusual crystalline structures that bestow on them unique chemical properties. They consist of a tetrahedral network of silicates and aluminum to form an aluminosilicate. The result is an extended honeycomb of channels and cavities. In one gram of zeolite, the channels provide up to several hundred square meters of surface area on which chemical reactions can take place. Zeolites can adsorb huge amounts of gas. Natural zeolites can adsorb up to 30% of their dry weight of the gases nitrogen and ammonia. That property suggests zeolites would be an excellent rock powder to incorporate into manure piles and early compost to soak up ammonia which would otherwise be lost to the atmosphere. I have known several dairy farmers who kept bulk rock phosphate in their barns to sprinkle over the fresh manure in the loafing areas each day. This usage serves a double purpose. It soaks up free ammonia and later on—as the manure is collected and spread in the fields—phosphorous is provided in a more available form.

Japanese farmers suspend boxes containing zeolites over their animals to improve herd health. Although this is an excellent practice, I doubt that farmers know what is happening. Zeolite rock powders are paramagnetic, and therefore are drawing down cosmic forces which then pass through the animals and into the soil. Those cosmic forces are health promoting, much like the healing clays. Farmers who are interested in trying out this practice would not have to find a zeolite rock powder, but could substitute a paramagnetic clay or a "lime."

The capacity of natural zeolites to take in large quantities of water even when humidity is low means they are deliquescent, and therefore, are good drying agents. They work better than traditional desiccants. In Japan, farmers use natural zeolites to dry animal feeds and fertilizers. This property suggests several uses. All too often a farmer is forced by weather conditions to put up hay that is too moist. Why not throw in a little zeolite as the hay is being put up to soak up much of the unwanted moisture? Of course, the question could be asked, *What happens to the animals that eat hay dusted with zeolite?* Many of the paramagnetic rock powders are beneficial to animals. I would be willing to chance it. But, of course, each farmer must make his or her own decision.

If the zeolites soak up moisture even in dry weather, wouldn't it be beneficial to have zeolite in the soil to carry crops through summer droughts? As an added incentive, zeolites with their very high cation exchange capacity should help construct a higher CEC for the soil.

When zeolites take on moisture, they produce warmth. When they lose moisture, they become cool. They are a natural temperature maintenance oven. Whether this property would have any significance in a soil system, I do not know. I merely mention it as something to be considered.

Recently, a Swedish study revealed that a natural zeolite, mordenite, decontaminated live animals and meat contaminated by the Chernobyl disaster. This further explains why the Lubkes of Austria were able to market their produce as contamination-free. Although the Lubkes did not use zeolites, their soils have properties that behaved in a similar fashion.

Certainly, zeolites can improve the quality of agricultural land. For more than one hundred years, Japanese farmers have improved their impoverished, acidic, sandy soils by spreading crushed rocks rich in zeolite. Because zeolites are such excellent ion exchangers, they help soils retain important nutrients, such as potash and nitrogen. This, combined with the capacity for holding water, prevents potassium, nitrates and ammonium ions from escaping and leaching into rivers. When used in combination with raw manure, ammonium salts, or urea, zeolites control the release of nitrogen allowing it to become available to plants over a sustained period of time, preventing damage by so-called "nitrogen burn." Natural zeolites also can make phosphorus in the soil more available to plants.

The first investigations of the effects of zeolites on animal nutrition were conducted in Japan in the 1960s. Later, investigators in the Soviet Union, Bulgaria, Cuba, Czechoslovakia, the United States and other countries validated the earlier findings. Most of the feed supplement experiments used were used primarily clinoptilolite zeolite, but mordenite was also tested. The results of these experiments revealed that when zeolites were added to the feed of poultry, swine, and cattle, they contributed to better digestion, increased weight gain, prevention and cure of diseases of the digestive tract, decrease of expenditures for medical service, control of offensive odors for excrement, decrease of feed-conversion values, higher animal survival rate, and elimination of mold during storage.

Nature's largess has given us zeolite minerals and endowed them with paramagnetic qualities. It is up to us to find out how we might benefit from them.

8

ENLIVENING
AND BALANCING THE SOIL

Man has two nervous systems. One is the craniosacral or parasympathetic system. It has two parts, the cranial and the sacrum. The cranial contains the brain. The sacrum is the bottom bone of the spinal column. The second nervous system is the thoracolumbar or sympathetic nervous system. It is based in the spinal column. This explanation oversimplifies some rather complicated physiology, yet it contains the general idea, which—for now—is sufficient. The functions of these two systems are usually antagonistic. A few examples of the antagonistic actions of these two system are listed so that results following stimulus may be compared.

Craniosacral Parasympathetic	Thoracolumbar Sympathetic
Contracts eye pupils	Dilates eye pupils
Slows heart action	Quickens heart action
Slows breathing	Quickens breathing
Increases glandular secretions	Decreases glandular secretions

For now it will be enough to relate this system to our solar system. After all, we have heard "As above, so below," and

"The universe is the macrocosm and man is the microcosm." The far planets, Mars, Jupiter and Saturn, acting through the agency of the Sun, make their influence felt via the silica in our soils and the flowers of our plants. The far planets, Mars, Jupiter and Saturn, also acting through the Sun, perform their task through the head and the base of the spinal column. We are required to consider the lenses of the eyes and their high silica content.

In a similar fashion, the near planets, Mercury, Venus and the Moon, acting through the Sun, have their chief influence on the leaf area of plants. In a parallel fashion, Mercury, Venus and the Moon, also, acting through the Sun, work most strongly on the spinal column.

Thus we have two distinct nervous systems of man, which are polarities in the same manner as the far planets, Mars, Jupiter and Saturn are polaric to the near planets of Mercury, Venus and the Moon. The nervous system of the human body is very complex. It is an electrical system in every sense of the word. Both positive and negative electricity are part of this system. The nerves are the conductors. They are insulated with myelin sheaths much as electrical wires have rubber or plastic insulation. If the insulation of a wire is damaged, a short may occur, shutting down the system. If the myelin sheath of a nerve is damaged or destroyed by disease, a short may occur, resulting in a severe disorder. Polio is just one of many disorders caused by the destruction of the myelin sheaths. Guillain-Barre syndrome is another. Our two nervous systems are polarities and must be kept insulated from each other. The craniosacral system is nourished by foods rich in silica such as the root crops. The thoracolumbar system is nourished by green leafy vegetables rich in "lime." In this way we can trace the polarity of our solar system through our soils,

LIVING PLANET

Earth is not a planet with life on it; rather it is a living planet. The physical structure of the planet—its core, mantle, and mountain ranges—acts as the skeleton or frame of its existence. The soil that covers its grasslands and forests is like a mammoth digestive system. In it all things are broken down, absorbed, and recycled into new growth. The oceans, waterways, and rain function as a circulatory system that moves life-giving "blood," purifying and revitalizing the body. The bacteria, algae, plants, and trees provide the planet's lungs, constantly regenerating the entire atmosphere. The animal kingdom provides the functions of a nervous system, a finely tuned and diversified series of organisms sensitized to environmental change. Each species is a unique expression of life, with its own unique consciousness and its own unique gifts to the body. Humanity allows the planet to exercise self-conscious awareness, or reflexive thought. That is, the human enables Earth to reflect on itself and on the divine mystery out of which it has come and in which it exists. We are a means by which nature can appreciate its own beauty and feel its own splendor; or destroy itself.

This shift, from seeing ourselves as separate beings placed on Earth ("the world was made for us") to seeing ourselves as a self-reflexive expression of Earth ("we were made for the world"), is a major shift in our understanding of who and what we are. It is a shift at the deepest possible level: our identity, or sense of self.

> —*Michael Dowd*
> *in a monograph,* The Big Picture

through our foods and right into our physiological makeup.

Let's try to trace the polarity of the solar system through the plant kingdom, using a tree as a representative genus specie. The living growing cells in the tree trunk are the cambium cells of the cambium layer. On the inner surface of the cambium are the xylem cells, which have the form of tubes. These tubes take up water and minerals from the roots to the aerial parts of the tree. The far planets, Mars, Jupiter and Saturn, working through the agent Sun and the silica of the soil, accomplish this task. If you will refer back to the chapter on silica and to one of the quotes from Rudolf Steiner, you will recall that, "All of these forces working inward from the Cosmos influence the growth of plants, not by direct radiation, but as follows. They are received by the Earth beneath its surface and from there are rayed upwards." This is levity, the polar force to gravity. Science knows nothing about levity because levity belongs to the spiritual world, and science—happy in its ignorance—does not recognize the spiritual world. This explains how water can be transported from the soil to the top of the highest tree. Science does not know how it is done and puts forward a number of ridiculous theories to explain the imponderable.

The near planets, Mercury, Venus and the Moon, working through the Sun and the "lime" of the soil, support the photosynthesis of leaves and the creation of sugars and starches which feed the tree. Sugars and starches are transported to the roots by the phloem cells, which are also in the form of tubes or pipes. Phloem cells are on the outer side of the cambium layer. In other words, the cambium layer is the insulation between two systems even as myelin sheaths are the insulators between the two nervous systems of the human body.

A perfect illustration of how these two forces work is found in the maple sap run in early spring. In northern Ohio, for instance, we have many sugar bush camps which support activity in the months of February and March making maple syrup. Maple sap runs best when days are warm and nights are cold. It takes Sun forces to get the sap running. The levity force of the Sun and far planets takes the sap up into the tree. The gravity force of the Sun and near planets brings it back down. The tap is inserted into the tree so that it intersects phloem cells to bring the sap down. I have worked with maple syrup, never too successfully, until the temperature reached about 45°. A better run was achieved generally on sunny days as opposed to cloudy ones. Maple syrup has to be made before the buds start swelling. When the buds start swelling the flavor is spoiled.

We have now discerned two polaric forces working in our solar system, in planet Earth, in man and in the plant kingdom. How about the soil? Did you ever hear anyone speak of two polaric systems in the soil?

We glibly talk about balancing our soils. But we are required to ask, specifically, just what is it that is being balanced? One answer might be balancing acid against alkaline. Balancing implies that there are two weights or two forces or two values or some norm which should be answered via adjustments. There is, of course, a perfect answer for the question if one realizes that there should be two polaric forces in the soil, and if one of the forces is weak, it should be strengthened to be in balance with the other. This is a brand new approach, for which reason there are no pat answers yet. We are going to be feeling our way for a long time.

But we do need two polaric forces in soils, paramagnetic and diamagnetic, and they should be in balance. We have seen that when there are two polaric forces, there has to be an insulating material between them, otherwise they short circuit. The insulating material in the soil is called organic matter. We rate organic matter, humus and humates on an ascending scale in their efficiency. Humates are what we should aim for, but we settle for just plain old organic matter. It takes a minimum of 2.5% organic matter to handle this insulation function, but we should aim for 3.5% organic matter in order to have a little better than adequate insulation. That is the first step in balancing a soil—get that organic matter up there where it ought to be.

I prefer to assume that the farmer has discontinued using salt fertilizer, otherwise he is beaten before he gets started. An explanation is in order. When a salt fertilizer dissolves in water, an ionic solution capable of conducting electricity is formed. This erases all insulation and eliminates any chance of balancing the forces in terms of which we speak. Thus we can add one more evil to a large inventory of evils associated with chemical salt fertilizers.

"Lime" is the material that can bring to the soil the diamagnetic forces. Most farmers have a philosophy regarding liming the soil, either to background how much lime to use, how to use it, or not to use it at all. For now it is sufficient to say that if the soil does not have sufficient "lime," then there is no chance whatsoever of balancing the soil. The farmer can work at the two goals simultaneously, bringing up organic matter and liming the soil. In fact, liming the soil will help greatly in bringing up the organic matter. The farmer is then ready to proceed to the material which will bring up the paramagnetic forces in the soil— namely the silica rock powders and/or the clay rock powders—but further consideration of the subject requires me to quote Steiner.

LIFE'S WAY

As the ice disappeared life found its way into this strange landscape. Vegetation gradually took over the newly exposed ground, enabling animal immigrants to survive. The animals, especially the large mammals, would have been as unfamiliar as the scenery to modern eyes. Mastodons, mammoths, saber-tooth cats, and giant short-faced bears were among the most spectacular. The small human population of 10,000 years ago may be to blame, at least in part, for their extinction. Our continent is the poorer for their disappearance; a knowledge of what we have lost should spur us to greater efforts to protect what remains; the grizzly bears, polar bears, cougars, big-horns, and other species that still survive, precariously, in what wild land remains to us.

—*E.C. Piglou,*
in After the Ice Age

"But we shall need something to attract the silica from the whole cosmic environment, for we must have this silica in the plant. Precisely, with regard to silica, the Earth gradually loses its power in the course of time. It loses it very slowly, therefore we do not notice it. This silica is of great importance." And I could add that this loss of silica in the soil is exactly why we have so many insect problems, disease problems, more susceptibility to winter kill, frost damage, loss of trees, etc.

With 27% silica in the Earth's crust, how could we be running short of silica? We aren't running short of silica, *per se*. We are losing the paramagnetic properties that silica is supposed to carry. Chemical agriculture is deadly to paramagnetic forces. But so far scientists seem not to have caught chemical agriculture with the smoking gun.

There are additional ways to restore paramagnetism to the soil, but first we need to balance the soil in terms of the parameters noted above.

A number of fine materials on the market carry paramagnetic forces. The suppliers' recommendations on the amount to use should be followed. Almost all will recommend around 400 or 500 pounds per acre. There may be a margin of safety in this. Still, in several instances, I applied well over a ton per acre without overloading my soil.

Let's say you now have brought the organic matter up to par in your soil. You've applied lime to bring the calcium value up to your desired level, and you have added paramagnetic rock dust. Theoretically, your soil should be balanced. But is it? Probably not. But you have made a good start, and in time you will get a feel for it and achieve the goal of getting your soil in balance. In achieving this type of soil balance you will have enlivened the soil.

There is no practical instrumentation for determining the

paramagnetic and diamagnetic properties of a soil. But this shortfall will be corrected in the fullness of time. Certainly such instrumentation should be helpful. A good dowser can determine the status of balance, however.

Several anecdotes are now of maximum interest. Maynard Murray, M.D., was puzzled as to why the sea mammals never contracted cancer. He thought that if he could find this answer, he could find a cure to that degenerative metabolic disorder. Accordingly, he worked tirelessly with sea salts. There is a bay in Baja, Mexico where the sea water gets trapped at high tide once a year. Over a period of time, the water evaporates and salts can be collected in commercial quantities. Sea salt should contain all the trace minerals found in the sea, which is all of them, so I bought half a ton of the sea salts from one of Murray's agents and spread it on my land. There went the paramagnetic forces on my land. I created an ionic situation which shorted out the forces. Nature is very forgiving and in due time the land recovered its forces. Never again did I apply a soluble salt material, to my land. For those who like to use sugar solutions or fish emulsions, they should be fine because they are not ionic and their solutions will not carry electrical currents. Solutions which will not carry electrical currents should pass muster, but stay away from solutions that will carry electrical currents.

I also did some consulting for organic farmers while working at the Brookside Laboratory. I well remember two farmers applying both rock phosphate and greensand at the same time. Instead of benefiting, the crops suffered badly. Rock phosphate and greensand are antagonistic to each other. Either, if applied by itself, works well, but when applied together they not only cancel each other out, they damage crops as well. The lesson to be learned here is to apply not more than one rock powder a year. The second year after this poor combination was applied the crops recovered and performed well. The antagonism had faded away. I have seen soil amendments in which a number of materials were mixed. Little or no thought was given to their compatibilities. With rare exceptions, this error costs the farmer the profit from his crop.

Recently, I was reviewing some old *Acres U.S.A.* articles. I came across *Mineralization in Kentucky* in the February 1972 issue. Field corn was grown on acres that had been mineralized for fifteen years. In some areas the corn was luxurious. In other areas the corn was normal. And in still other areas the corn plants died early. Why the great variation? The answer, now seemingly obvious, was discovered and quantified by Phil Callahan. Some of the minerals were paramagnetic and some were diamagnetic. Depending upon how these minerals got mixed in the field, the areas were either in very good balance, average balance, or the forces were canceled out. Since the details of the experiment are no longer available, further comment is useless. But the bottom line remains the same. If the farmer will use only one mineral per year and give it a chance to be digested by the soil, the soil will be a beneficiary.

9

SUSTAINABLE AGRICULTURE

Sustainable agriculture has become a well recognized buzz word. The movement took form in organiculture immediately after World War II, supported by the Rodale journal, *Organic Farming & Gardening*. J.I. Rodale became the chief publicist with his little magazine. Rodale was essentially an industrialist. During the first few years of his publishing career, he relied on Sir Albert Howard and Ehrenfried Pfeiffer for his guidance. Sir Albert Howard, an Englishman, and Ehrenfried Pfeiffer, a Swiss, both had long and varied experiences in the organic field. Pfeiffer had studied and worked under Rudolf Steiner, thus in a very real sense what goes around comes around. Much of what Steiner taught in 1924 came around full circle with the birth of the organic movement in 1944. Gradually the movement assumed American overtones. Under the tutelage of William A. Albrecht, Joseph Cocannouer, Louis Bromfield, Royal Lee, Joe Nichols, Jonathan Foreman, Samuel Hood and dozens more, the movement pulled the fledgling idea to its feet by its own bootstraps.

All along, there have been many who disliked the name *organic farming*. Others came along and supplied a new spin: eco-farming, biological farming, alternative agriculture, regenerative agriculture, and now sustainable farming. The terms haven't made much difference to me. I could live with any of them since their intent is the same, production of safe quality food without contamination of soil and water

THE NILE

Thundering, a shining sheet of water, radiantly blue, tense with life, plunges round the reef of a rocky islet in a double fall, while below, the spray thickens in a milky green vortex, madly whirling its won foam to an unknown destiny. In such clamour, the Nile is born.

In a quiet inlet at the edge of the mighty fall, a gigantic maw yawns pink. Puffing and sluggish, the hippopotamus snorts and grunts as it raises its head above the water to squirt a water jet from its nostrils between its pink-lined ears. Lower down, where the water grows calmer, bronze-green dragons, with black spots on their carapace and a yellowish belly, lie basking; to complete the illusion of fairyland, their eyes are rimmed with gold. Each bears a bird on its back, or even between its teeth, for the dragon sleeps open-mouthed. This is Leviathan from the *Book of Job*, the crocodile. It looks like some strange survival from the time when ferns and forests covered the earth and saurians ruled the world.

—*Emil Ludwig*
in The Nile

resources. *Sustainable farming* seems to have the nod these days.

When I think of sustainable farming I think of the Egyptians whose lifeline was the Nile River. Up to the construction of the High Aswan Dam, Egypt logged in over 6,000 years of sustainable farming, and if properly analyzed, this record has to contain valid lessons. Much like our own, their farming methods are suspect, but the fortuitous circumstances under which they farmed merit attention. Their Egyptian gods smiled upon them.

The Nile River has two main tributaries, the White Nile, which has its source in the lowlands of Sudan, with its wealth of paramagnetic stone dusts, and the Blue Nile, which has its source at Lake Victoria in Ethiopia, which always furnishes a flush of organic matter. Each year the Nile River flooded the Delta, depositing sediments rich in organic matter and enlivened rock powders. It may be an oversimplification to say an annual application of organic matter and rock powders is the answer to sustainable agriculture but, basically, that is the answer. We must keep a high level of organic matter in our soils along with a good balance of enlivened rock powders. With this combination we should be able to carry on our agriculture for 6,000 years, or at least until the next ice age arrives.

I was with the *Acres U.S.A.* group that toured Egypt in 1984. Phil Callahan was one of the leaders of our party, and I well remember him saying that the sand on the west bank of the Nile was paramagnetic, whereas the sand on the east bank was diamagnetic. Not that I didn't believe him, but I had to test it for myself. Of course he was right. Those Egyptian soils were highly enlivened, i.e., they were either paramagnetic or diamagnetic depending upon where they were found. I also remember the oranges served to us on

ANCIENT WISDOM

The scientific system cannot function without additivety, namely, units of measurement that have equal intervals and an absolute zero. As we consider these ideas, history soon enough enters the picture, and so does one of man's first intellectual pursuits. This business of units for measurements goes back to the cradle of agriculture and a symbol one finds ten miles west of the modern city of Cairo. At the end of an acacia, tamarind and eucalyptus lined avenue lies the rocky plateau of Giza. It is a mile square, and from a height of 130 feet it dominates the palm groves of the Nile Valley. On this man-leveled plateau stands the great pyramid of Cheops. West lies the Libyan desert.

The great pyramid covers thirteen acres, or about seven midtown blocks in the city of New York. From this huge area, leveled to within a fraction of an inch, more than two and a half million limestone and granite blocks rise in 201 stepped tiers to a height of forty stories. These blocks weigh from two to seventy tons, the biggest being as heavy as a modern locomotive engine.

Time has taken most of the records associated with the enterprise, but we do know that whoever built the great pyramid knew the dimensions of this planet as they were not known again until the seventeenth century. By observing the stars, these builders could and did measure the day, the year, the hour, the minute, the second. They linked time with distance because they knew a circle had 360° and accordingly they computed longitude and latitude, the distance from pole to pole, from earth to sun, and the exact equator. They graduated distances into exact units called cubit and foot, and no man could tamper with these measures because they were fixed by the vault of the heavens and recorded in the dimensions of the great pyramid.

In mathematics these ancients were advanced enough to have discovered the function of pi and Fibonacci's series. The record they left in deathless stone reveals that Eratosthenes was not the first to measure the circumference of the Earth, Hipparchus was not the first to understand trigonometry, Pythagoras was not the first to originate his theorem, and Mercator was not the first to invent that projection.

The ancients also knew about dilution and delivering a uniform nutrient fix to their Delta acres. One marvels at how nearly they approximated Dan Skow's distribution of atoms over acres, having first harvested carbon and paramagnetic stone from the Blue and White Nile.

   —*Charles Walters*
   in the Foreword to Mainline Farming
   for Century 21

that trip. I have never eaten such delicious oranges. In fact, the entire trip was a gastronomic delight. The flavor in other foods was outstanding.

The CEC (cation exchange capacity) of any soil is just about the most meaningful value found in any soil report. It tells the farmer what the potential productivity of his soil is. Another way of looking at the CEC is the potential fertility of the soil. For a sandy soil, the CEC might run as high as 10. For a clay soil it could run as high as 20. I worked in a soil testing laboratory for nearly ten years and rarely saw a CEC over 20. Any CEC over 20 signifies a very high potential fertility. Yet the CEC of two Egyptian soils I tested ran 42 and 45 respectively. That is mind-boggling. What is the secret of those Egyptian soils?

It may be enough to say, *They are humates.* What are humates? Because of its acid properties, humic acid (or humus) in soils with adequate lime will combine with the lime to form humates. Soils rich in humates are extremely fertile. A soil can be rich in humus, but if it is lacking in lime it will not be a fertile soil. Too many soils in our country fall into this category. Or we can change the formula around and have a soil rich in minerals or lime but lacking in humus. Such a soil is infertile. Unfortunately there is a perception among many organic farmers that if they will add minerals or rock powders to their land, it will become fertile. In fact, if they do not have the humus to go with the rock powders, they will be disappointed. Cliff Myer, a salesman for Planters Soil Conditioner, told me about taking a load of his material to a cotton farm in North Carolina. Those acres had been cotton and tobacco farmed for two hundred years. The organic matter in that soil was practically zero and the results were near absolute zero. Planters Soil Conditioner is a good material, but nothing is going to work in a soil that has little or no organic matter.

Sustainable agriculture on actively cultivated land is possible only when humus and rock powders are supplied year after year, every year, even as the Nile River supplied the Delta with its fresh supply of humus and rock powders every year or two. Pastures, orchards and other land not actively cultivated every year may be an exception. Supplying these materials each annum is probably the biggest problem in sustainable agriculture. Can a farmer farming one thousand acres do a good job of sustainable farming. My answer would have to be, *No!* Can a farmer farming one hundred acres do a good job? Not likely. The concept of larger and larger farms is completely at odds with the concept of sustainable agriculture. The Egyptian farmer is limited to fifty acres by law. He might be a millionaire, but he still cannot buy more than fifty acres. The Swiss farms are about twenty five acres in size, and they support their operators nicely. The time has come to downsize our American farms—if we expect them to be viable for 6,000 years.

Do I practice what I preach? Yes. I am just a farmer-gardener with one large and one small plot. Each year I spread my Biodynamic compost and a rock powder over both areas. I experiment with different rock powders because they are my "thing." I have used Clod Buster, basalt, Nutri-Carb, Azomite, Flora-Stim, lime, gypsum, rock phosphate, diatomaceous earth, Planters Soil Conditioner, ProMin, and others. They all have done a good job for me and I don't hesitate to recommend any of them. My gardens produce well regardless of the weather. It may be a drought year or a wet year or unseasonably hot or cool, it doesn't make much difference. My soil is making humates, the same stuff so characteristic of Egyptian soils, except their soils are 6,000 years ahead of mine and much more fertile. I don't expect to catch up with the Egyptian soils, but it is fun trying.

The Egyptian soils have the most beautiful crumb structure I have ever seen. Break up a clod of their soil and it breaks into thousands of crumbs along fracture lines. Unfortunately, with the damming of the Nile River at the High Aswan Dam, there will be no more flooding of the Nile River valley, and no annual deposit of humus and minerals. Their soils are already turning white with salt buildup, and what took 6,000 years to build up may not take more than sixty years to break down.

If you are working with rock powders you should know a little something about the transmutation of elements. This is a subject science avoids since its practitioners know so little about it, and yet it happens continuously in the mineral, plant, animal and human kingdoms. Therefore, transmutation is not hard to understand if you consider the elements not so much material as spiritual with strong enzymatic forces. Transmutation is not so much a chemical reaction as a spiritual digestion.

The name of Louis Kervran is synonymous with the subject of biological transmutation, for which reason I now direct attention to his observations. As a youngster he noted that the chickens which his folks kept picked up pieces of mica grit found in the yard. When the chickens were butchered and the gizzards inspected, the mica grit was not to be found. Presumedly it had been digested. There was no lime grit given to the chickens and yet their eggs have strong calcareous shells. It wasn't until later in life that he determined the silica in the micra grit had transmuted to the calcium found in the shells.

How many of us have wondered where dairy cows get the calcium they require? Many dairy cows give at least

20,000 pounds of milk a year. They give birth to a calf weighing from seventy five to ninety pounds and at the same time keep up their own calcium metabolism. It doesn't take an expert in nutrition to tell us that those cows are putting out more calcium than they are taking in. Where is that extra calcium coming from? At the same time they are eating pasture grasses, hay, corn silage and grains, all rich in silica. The extra calcium they require is coming from the silica they are taking in. The silica is transmuting to calcium.

Silica has an atomic weight of 28. Carbon has an atomic weight of 12. Add the two together and you get 40 which is the atomic weight of the calcium. Sounds simple, but it is more complex than we can fully understand.

A similar phenomenon takes place in my compost pile. While I am building up the pile, I work in basalt which is a grey powder. After several months in the compost pile, I notice the basalt powder has turned white and is now lime. No one can tell me I may be mistaken because I am a chemist, and I have tested that white material carefully. It is lime. It is not only lime, it is nascent lime. The word *nascent* comes from the Latin, meaning "in the act of being born." This nascent lime is much more active than regular lime. It will combine with humic acid to form humate, which is a highly desirable end product. Other silica rock powders should act in a similar fashion, although I have not made the confirming observation as I have with basalt. Of course, the sure fire way of producing a humate in the compost pile is to add a little lime during the site's construction. By adding a rock powder to the compost pile, you are adding another dimension, enhancing the properties of the compost as you add it to your gardens or fields or fruit trees.

The Nile River serves Egypt by trundling minerals as far north as the Mediterranean via the agency of silica rock powders. The minerals come from the mountains of Ethiopia. They are granite, feldspar, mica and quartz, which are parent materials for the African mountains. These minerals are deposited on the land along with the humus. This means that there was a type of composting going on right in the soil. Nature was transmuting some of the silica to lime to humates. Can we compost the rock powders and humus right in the soil, bypassing the compost pile? Perhaps. Such a process would be a form of sheet composting.

If you have followed me, you will know that I use the rock powders annually. I place them in my compost pile and also spread them directly on the land along with my compost. I use a rototiller to incorporate both the compost and the rock powders into the soil simultaneously. That is my entire fertilizer program. It has been my program for many years and will remain so for years to come.

Before we leave the subject of transmutation, let's hear what Rudolf Steiner has to say on the subject. "For there is a hidden alchemy in the organic process. This hidden alchemy transmutes potash into nitrogen, provided that the potash is working properly in the organic process. Nay more, it even transmutes into nitrogen the lime if it is working rightly."

So many gardeners and farmers in the organic movement are fearful their crops will suffer a nitrogen deficiency. We have to have faith that nature in her infinite wisdom has her ways of providing nitrogen, but we must learn how to work with her, not against her.

10

SOIL STRUCTURE , DROUGHT, COLD, INSECT AND DISEASE RESISTANCE

The title to this chapter appears to cover a wide range of topics, but at the end you will realize they are all interrelated. Troubles start at the ground level and work up. The way to get rid of the troubles is to start at ground level and that is what I do with soil structure.

Our Earth is a living entity. It breathes and has a fluid circulation system along with the other systems necessary for life. Certainly, everyone must have been on a lake or river early in the morning and witnessed the mists rising and gradually dissipating as the morning wore on. In the evening we witness the mists starting to collect and then slowly settle in as night fell. That is one of the pleasures in fishing early in the morning or late in the day. In the morning we witness the Earth as she is breathing out and in the evening we witness the Earth as she is breathing in. The Earth takes a full breath once every twenty four hours. It is exactly the same phenomenon as occurs in the maple tree referred to in an earlier chapter. As the Sun rises and silica forces predominate, sap rises in the tree and the mists rise up from the lake. As the Sun sets and "lime" forces predominate, the sap falls in the tree and mists settle on the lake.

The same phenomenon should take place in the soil. The

HUMATES

A humate is a salt form of humic acids. "Humus is the organic matter of soils that has decayed sufficiently to have lost its identity with regards to its origin. The most important and biochemically active group of the many degradation products of soil organic materials is the alkalisoluble fraction commonly called the humic acids. The salts of these humic acids are known as the humates. The ability of the humates to poise or regulate water-holding capacity or content is probably their most significant property so far as agriculture is concerned, since from a quantitative point water is the most important plant material derived from the soil. In conjunction with this water regulating effect, the humates possess extremely high ion exchange capacities, and it is this property that makes possible better retention and utilization of fertilizers by preventing excessive leaching away from the root zones and ultimately releasing them to the growing plants as needed. The humates reduce soil erosion by increasing the cohesive forces of the very fine soil particles. The desirable friable character of fertile soils is maintained through the formation of colloidal mineral complexes, which assist in aeration and the prevention of large clods and stratification. Very low concentrations of purified humates have been shown to stimulate seed germination and viability, root growth, especially lengthwise. Significantly increased yields have been reported for many crops, such as cotton, potatoes, wheat, tomatoes, mustard, and nursery stock. They have also been shown to stimulate growth and proliferation of desirable soil microorganisms as well as algae and yeasts. A number of workers have reported that the humic acids can solubilize and make available to plants certain materials that are otherwise unavailable, such as rock phosphates. The humates seem to play an important role in plant utilization and metabolism of the phosphates. The humic acids apparently can liberate carbon dioxide from soil calcium carbonates and thus make it available to the plant through the roots for photosynthesis. The humates are known to stimulate plant enzymes. The humates...are nature's soil conditioners par excellence." (Humate materials are also known as Leonardite.)

—*Everette M. Burdick,*
in Economic Botany

moisture in the soil should rise in the morning and fall in the evening. But this phenomenon depends upon the soil's being paramagnetic. If the soil has lost its paramagnetism, there is no movement of soil moisture. We have blamed the loss of soil structure on plowing with its resulting plow soles, upon heavy farm machinery moving over the land, upon the use of chemicals with their deleterious effects on soil life, upon monoculture, all of which are true. But I never hear mention of the fact that soil loses its structure due to the loss of paramagnetism.

The evidence is overwhelming that paramagnetism in the soil is necessary for good soil structure, forgetting for the moment the correction of the other problems mentioned. The best soil structure I ever saw was in those Egyptian soils with their very high paramagnetism. Those soils broke up into small crumbs, each crumb looking like a tiny crystal. Garnet Strite and his son, Larry, showed me how the use of FloraStim, a paramagnetic clay, restored soil structure to some of the farmland in Pennsylvania. We could take a three-eighths inch iron bar and thrust in three feet into the soil with only hand pressure. Leland Taylor has written many articles for both his own newsletter and for *Acres U.S.A.* on the use of Clod Buster, a paramagnetic silica powder which has restored the soil structure on many farms. I have seen how the use of paramagnetic rock powders and Biodynamics have restored the soil structure on my farm, which was a grain farm before I bought it. How does that happen?

Can you visualize how dynamic moisture circulation in the soil would gradually arrange or rearrange the soil particles to improve structure? I acknowledge that there are other factors involved in arriving at structure maintenance, but I can't think of anything more important than good moisture circulation. Consider a soil with stagnant moisture and compare it to a stagnant pond of water. What does a stagnant pond of water breed? It breeds mosquitos, fungal growths and disease. Stagnant moisture in the soil is not going to breed mosquitos, but it could breed undesirable insects, molds and diseases. Good moisture circulation in the soil will promote good air circulation. Just look back at those mists rising and falling over the lake. Those mists were not water alone, but a water and air mixture.

We are now ready to proceed to drought resistance. Let us assume that our soil has 2.5% to 3.5% or more organic matter and is balanced between the paramagnetic and diamagnetic forces. We will further assume that we are in a drought period and soil moisture is falling. Nevertheless, there is still some moisture deep down in the soil and it rises every morning where the crops gain access to some of it. The crops so dependent are not the best, but neither are they the worst and they will make a little money.

A few years ago we had a terrible drought settle in over northern Ohio, possibly the worst in the nation. We went three months with no rain and for two weeks the temperature never fell below 90°F. For a few days it was over 100°F, and one day it got up to 105°F. In spite of it all, my garden and orchard trees produced good crops. They didn't break any records, but they did produce. I have gotten to the point where I don't care much what the season is like. My garden and fruit trees will produce. There is a large woodlot in back of my land. During the 1988 drought, I would look at that woods and marvel at how green those trees remained. It wasn't just that woods, but most woods. I kept thinking that if the trees in that woods can stay so green, then my fruit trees should stay green as well. My fruit trees did stay green, but not quite as green as those trees in the woods. That soil in the woods was better than my soil.

Leland Taylor in his crusade against drought resistance has several special lessons to teach us. Leland drives about 50,000 miles a year inspecting the crops of his customers. He has seen droughts and their effects in the East, the South, the Midwest and the West. I well remember August 1983, a drought year in our section of Ohio. Leland had a farm meeting at Melvin Herschberger's place near Mount Eaton, Ohio. Melvin had very nice corn and alfalfa. In fact, he had already made three cuttings of alfalfa and was waiting for the meeting so the participants could inspect the alfalfa crop before he cut it again. Most farmers in the area weren't going to get more than two cuttings, yet there was Melvin getting four cuttings. Needless to say, his soil had very good paramagnetic properties. The rock powder was Clod Buster.

We are now ready to proceed to cold resistance and again we will find the answer in the soil. I will start with my own experiences. Sweet cherry trees do not do very well in Ohio. The winters are too severe. If a young sweet cherry tree can be nursed along for the first four or five years, it may make it, but those first years are difficult. In my orchard I planted and replanted sweet cherry trees only to see them winterkill during one of their early winters. In the winter of 1986-1987 I had four young sweet cherry trees, all the same age, all planted in the same area of my orchard. All four went into the winter looking healthy, but when spring arrived three of them had winter killed. The fourth tree looked beautiful and has prospered ever since. What was different about that fourth tree? It was about twenty feet away from my Biodynamic compost pile, which radiates forces continuously. Those forces had been taken up by the sap in the tree. There was better circulation of the sap in that tree, for which reason the tree endured the hard winters. Paramagnetic forces and Biodynamic forces have some characteristics in common, so I figured that if the Biodynamic forces had pulled that tree through the winter I would really bear down hard on the paramagnetic forces and determine what results I could get with them. The soil organic matter was good, and I had limed the orchard. Therefore, its diamagnetic properties were good, but I hadn't done much about its paramagnetic properties. I made a heavy application of a silica rock powder, and that was the answer.

Another fruit crop, smoothstem blackberries, doesn't do well in northern Ohio and I had tried for years to raise them, only to see them winterkill. After winterkill, new shoots would come up in the spring. First year shoots don't produce berries. One doesn't get the berries until the second year. I had given up on them, abandoned them, but had not grubbed them out. The roots continued to shoot up new sprouts every year, only to die the following winter. After I spread the paramagnetic rock dust there was no more winterkill, and those smoothstem blackberries produce some of my nicest berries.

I have a cold frame along the south side of my house in which I raise salad greens all winter. They grow fine all winter. When the outside temperature drops to below zero, it may get as cold as 15°F or 20°F in the cold frame, but the salad greens keep right on growing. As I write these lines, the thermometer tells me it is the coldest night since the great blizzard of 1977. It is down to -15°F, but those salad greens are still green and look fine. I can't say they are happy, but neither have they expired. They will get back on track in several days. The soil in my cold frame has about 6% humates and is highly paramagnetic. I spread a heavy application of rock dust and Biodynamic compost on that bed every year. It must have the equivalent of five or ten

A DIFFERENT FORMULA

Occasionally we find in scientific literature a note to the effect that chemical fertilizers must be given in the correct proportions in accordance with soil analyses. But since, in most cases, a field is not uniform in soil content, we should, theoretically, have to use a different formula for each of its variations. That would be particularly difficult in soils that have been produced by weathering. As experts in the science of fertilizing themselves readily admit, this differentiation is, indeed, theoretically necessary, but impossible of practical application. Therefore, they take an averaged formula and accept unbalanced fertilizing as inevitable in practice.

In regions where enough moisture in the form of atmospheric humidity, sub-surface water and rain is available, fewer difficulties are encountered at first in respect of hardening and the alteration of the soil structure. This is because the normal admissible balance of mineral salts is again produced through the balancing, distributing and dissolving effect of the water.

In Holland, for example, the bad effects of artificial fertilizers appear much more slowly, because the high level and the constant circulation of the water table in Holland provide for a natural equalization. But what happens in a dry summer or in an arid climate? In addition to the crusting of the surface, another phenomenon may be observed. In a field will suddenly appear small, less fertile patches. These grow from year to year, and in dry years, there will be more and more of these sterile spots. We may ascribe these to so-called free acid products, that is, insoluble or practically insoluble silicates which are formed out of the soil silicates in the interchange of salts. These insoluble silicates must be regarded as lost to the substance cycle of agriculture, and can be won back only after a long organic "cure."

We should not precipitate the salts in our soil, but should rather open the soil and enliven it. The organic processes taking place in the soil due to light, air, weather, microscopic organisms and humus, are the activities that help its "demineralization" on the one side, and foster its "becoming organic" on the other. In so doing they open up extensive reserves. When, as a result of a single year's harvest, the soil substances are used up, new substances are again set free through the natural action of weathering in a living, vital soil. Tillage and the eroding effect of wind and water liberate new soil ingredients every year. These need only to be enriched, "organized" in the most literal sense of the word.

—*Ehrenfried Pfeifffer,*
as abstracted from Bio-Dynamic Farming and Gardening

tons per acre of paramagnetic rock dust on it. To anyone who has a cold frame, a hot bed or a greenhouse, I would say, *Get the paramagnetic forces as high as possible.* Don't be afraid to spread the rock powders on very heavily. It's the paramagnetic forces which keep the plant saps circulating and when there is a good circulation of the plant saps, there should be no winterkills.

One more story on cold resistance will illustrate some of the points I want to make. In my orchard I have 25 peach trees. Anyone with peach trees abhors those late spring frosts which kill the blossoms. No blossoms, no peaches. I can't say that all of my blossoms make it through those late spring frosts, but most of them do—and I always end up with a nice peach harvest.

We are now ready to proceed to disease resistance. There are so many plant diseases that many universities have entire departments devoted to plant pathology. The only aspect I will consider are those diseases that respond to paramagnetic rock powders and are circulatory in nature.

The classical story is the one related by Peter Tompkins, and Chris Bird in their book, *Secrets of the Soil*. There are many forests dying in Europe. One such forest is owned by Rudolf Schindele, who raises trees for their veneer. He observed that where his heavy log trucks rumbled through the forest raising clouds of dust, the trees were doing fine. He started producing the rock powder on a commercial scale and applying it to other forests where the trees were dying. Those trees recovered. He named the dust Biomin. A friend of mine in France sent me a sample which tested out just as I expected. It was a paramagnetic silica rock powder. When the circulation of the sap was restored, the trees recovered.

How many of our American trees are in trouble? The American chestnut is gone, the American elm, the red oaks, some of the maples and some of the pines have died or live on borrowed time. I think there are more. It seems that every year I hear of another tree in trouble. Let's hear once more from Rudolf Steiner: "But we shall need something to attract the silica from the whole scenic environment, for we must have this silica in the plant. Precisely, with regard to silica, the Earth gradually loses its power in the course of time. It loses it very slowly, therefore we do not notice it. This silica is of great importance." To which I could comment that the Earth is losing its power very quickly if the disease and death of trees is any indication.

Peak Minerals, Inc., which mines and promotes Azomite, sponsored research of diseases, citrus tree decline and peach tree short life syndrome. Two different diseases but basically, the same disease, a plugging of the vessels carrying the vital life forces of the tree, the sap. Here we go again— reduce the sap flow, and disease is the result. Azomite is a highly paramagnetic clay powder and also carries a large spectrum of trace minerals. The use of Azomite was successful in arresting the disease.

We are now ready to proceed to insect resistance. Organic farmers and gardeners know that their insect problems are fewer than those who use chemicals. There are several reasons. I will elaborate on only one of them. All living entities have magnetic fields, from the lowly bacteria to the mighty elephant. Some people refer to these magnetic fields as auras. You have an aura. I have an aura. If we have the paramagnetic forces working well in our gardens, fields and orchards, our garden crops, field crops and fruit harvest will display the forces of the soil in which they grow. If the force fields of the crops are antagonistic to the force fields of the insects, insects will leave. It is as simple as that.

The best example I can think of is on my own farm. There

was a time when the Japanese beetles were present in substantial numbers. The better I got my soils in balance, the fewer the beetles. There are only a handful of beetles on my farm anymore, and I can live with that. They just don't like the forces around here anymore.

Another example is the cabbage worm. We still have a few cabbage butterflies around, and I suppose they lay their eggs somewhere—but they don't lay their eggs on my cabbages. The cabbages now have a force field they don't like. Most of the insects which used to give us problems are now found in few numbers.

The worst insect pest for the fruit growers in the eastern United States is the plum curculio. There are no organic sprays I know of to control it. But the curculio has an Achilles heel, its force field. When we find a force field it doesn't like, that will end our problems with it.

To summarize. As you get your soils in good paramagnetic balance, the insects will diminish in numbers. To be more specific, both forces, paramagnetic and diamagnetic should be in balance. Some insects have paramagnetic forces and it takes the diamagnetic forces to chase them off. Other insects have diamagnetic forces and it takes the paramagnetic forces to chase them off.

11

ENZYMES, VITAMINS, MINERALS AND SUNSHINE

What are enzymes? Almost any standard English language dictionary defines enzymes as any of numerous proteins or conjugated proteins produced by living organisms and functioning as biochemical catalysts in living organisms. The key word here is *catalyst,* so back to the dictionary to find out what a catalyst is. "A substance usually present in small amounts relative to the reactants that modifies and increases the rate of a chemical reaction without being consumed in the process." Now, do you understand what an enzyme is? If you do, good for you, but do you understand how it works? The situation is somewhat like that surrounding the word *electricity.* We all know what electricity will do, but we don't know what electricity is. The same thing if true of enzymes. We know what enzymes will do, but we don't understand what they are.

The enzymologist classified enzymes as matter, but I contend that enzymes are forces. For electricity to manifest itself requires an electric motor or a light bulb. For wind power to manifest itself requires a windmill or a sailboat. For solar power to manifest requires growing crops. So it is with enzymes. For enzymes to manifest themselves, they need a material substance, a receiver. The material substance for many enzymes is a protein product, a combination of a protein with a mineral key. Our rock powders are minerals

TRACE NUTRIENTS

Gabriel Bertrand, a French scientist and the father of the study of trace elements, proposed a rule which we will call Bertrand's Law of *optimal nutritive concentration*. It states that in the absence of an essential element a plant cannot live. It thrives on adequate amounts, but an excess is toxic. He worked this out for manganese, but the principle applies not only to plants but to all animal life. Eugene D. Weinberg has discovered an extension of the Law which we will call Weinberg's Principle. He showed with certain bacteria and manganese that amounts adequate for growth were not necessarily adequate for optimal function—in this case the production of an antibiotic—and this Principle bears very important applications for the nutrition and health of all living things, especially us.

—*Henry A. Schroeder, M.D.*,
in The Trace Elements and Man

and they do encompass the necessary trace minerals for life such as iron, copper, cobalt, zinc, selenium, boron, manganese, molybdenum, and the "lime" minerals of calcium, magnesium, potassium and sodium. Without these minerals, there would be no enzymes and without enzymes life would be very difficult or impossible. Enzymes and minerals are two sides of the same coin. Without minerals there can be no enzymes and without enzymes the minerals would be hard put to perform their function. Going back to the definition of an enzyme, which calls for a biochemical catalyst, I claim the biochemical catalyst is the force contained in the mineral. The minerals could well be one of those contained in paramagnetic rock powders.

Enzymes start in the soil even as the minerals start in the soil. The enzymes along with their minerals work their way up to the plants and from there on up to the animals and man. If the soil has no enzymes, then the food grown on that soil lacks some vital life forces and the animal or the person who eats that food, will likewise lack vital life forces.

The enzymes discussed up to this point have been those associated with proteins and minerals. These enzymes are very sensitive to temperatures above 115°F to 120°F. Higher temperatures distort the protein chains which are the carriers of the enzymes. In that manner the enzymes are destroyed. This is the problem typified by the pasteurization of milk or cooking food. The enzymes are heat sensitive and destroyed, a process that is exacerbated if the source of heat is the microwave oven.

There are enzymes associated with silica. As pointed out earlier, the silica rock powders are polaric to the "lime" rock powders which encompass most of the trace minerals. The enzymes associated with silica are not as heat sensitive as those associated with the "lime" minerals. For example, I

ENZYME SYSTEMS

Plants rely on enzyme systems as regulated by their micronutrient keys. Here are a very few of these enzyme systems and their trace element keys.

Enzyme	Key
Nitrate reductase	Molybdenum
Gentanic dehydrogenase	Copper
Phospholipase	Manganese
Cytochrome	Iron
Starch phosphorylase	Boron
Auxin enzyme	Zinc, etc.

The enzymes are protein amino acid clusters. They speed up the rate of a specific chemical reaction in a plant. Each specific enzyme is tied to its individual chemical reaction. As a result, this necessary enzyme is produced in each plant cell at the time of cell division.

Each enzyme is inert and non-specific until activated by a specific trace element. This trace element is the key that unlocks enzymatic activity and fires it up so that it can do its work in the metabolic process. N, P and K are not taken up as plant nutrients except under enzymatic control. When this activity falters, the result is a cellular short circuit. This may mean less production, production without keeping quality, or a crop incapable of defending itself against insect, bacterial and fungal attack.

Trace minerals in a soil system can either vanish or become locked up as a result of imbalanced fertilization. This means return of trace minerals to the soil itself is fraught with unwanted possibilities, namely the new supply being promptly complexed and held unavailable. (It is the supreme role of enlivened rock powders to prevent this tragedy.)

—*Charles Walters and C.J. Fenzau*
in An Acres U.S.A. Primer

bake bread at 250°F and the silica enzymes are not destroyed. The silica enzymes evidently are those associated with the bran of the rye grains, since I bake rye bread. Those who bake bread generally bake it around 350°F for an hour. It takes my bread two and half hours to bake, but the enzymes are retained. The bread with its enzymes is easily digested and furnishes lots of energy. I am very particular that my rye is organically grown. The whole enzyme technology is tenuous and there is much more to be learned about it.

Another similar but nebulous subject is vitamins. Thousands of hours of research by hundreds by researchers have been spent on vitamin research, and still they are mysterious. Vitamins, like enzymes, are dependent upon minerals. Therefore paramagnetic rock powders could well play an essential role in their formation. The minerals found in vitamins are practically the same as those found in enzymes.

Vitamin A may be found in alfalfa, asparagus, broccoli, carrots, celery, chard, dandelion, escarole, horseradish, lettuce, parsley, peppers, sweet potatoes, spinach, squash, turnip greens, apricots, cherries, nectarines, peaches, prunes, butter, cheese, milk, eggs, fish oils and some meats. The story with the other vitamins is about the same. They are found in a wide variety of foods. Only one conclusion can be drawn. Vitamins are not something material; rather they are forces found in foods.

Another similarity of vitamins and enzymes is their susceptibility to heat. Some are susceptible and some are not. Vitamin A is not susceptible to heat. Foods containing vitamin A can be boiled without destroying them. Vitamin B has its own set of revelations. There are so many modifications of this vitamin that only a general statement can be made that ordinary cooking does not destroy it. Vitamin C is sensitive to heat. It cannot survive cooking. Vitamin D is not heat sensitive. Taking vitamins as a whole, there are so many conditions which have a bearing such as boiling in the presence of air, boiling not in the presence of air, steaming, acid or alkaline, cooking in copper kettles, that definite conclusions simply cannot be reached.

The simplest vitamin of all is vitamin D, the sunshine vitamin. All you have to do to take in vitamin D is to get out in the Sun. There can be no doubt that vitamin D is not a material, but a force. And so I make my claim that vitamins, like enzymes, are forces, and foods are their carriers. Where does one find forces? The Ultimate force is the Sun, but Sun forces can be modified in many ways by planets, the constellations and the Moon.

Another facet of vitamins rarely mentioned is that manures can be rich in vitamins. As the manures are composted and returned to the soil, the soil, too, can be enriched by the vitamins. Nature is the ultimate recycler. Nothing is wasted. All is recycled. As we learn to work with nature, more vitamins will be made available to us.

Another approach to vitamins is to consider them as life forces. Edward Bach developed what he termed "flower remedies." In his lifetime, which was short 1888 - 1936, he developed thirty-seven flower and one rock remedy for a total of thirty-eight. Twenty of these valid health remedies are activated by the Sun and eighteen by boiling water. Here we have another statement on heat sensitivity. Could it be that each flower remedy might be considered a life force and thus a vitamin?

The word *vitamins* derived from *vita*, meaning life, and *amine* is any of a group of organic compounds containing nitrogen. What does Steiner have to say about nitrogen?

"Everywhere, in the animal kingdom and in the plant and even in the soil, the bridge between carbon and oxygen is afforded by nitrogen. Nitrogen is the mediator. Nitrogen guides life into form. Nitrogen is the astral element." The definition of a vitamin could thus be a vital life force found in foods or flowers mediated by nitrogenous compounds, nitrogen being an astral element. I would summarize by saying that the use of paramagnetic rock powders in our agriculture could do no less than enhance the vitamins in our foods.

12

BREAD FROM STONES

Now we come to the bottom line—our health. A healthy soil, healthy plants and healthy animals are all fine, but what about human health? My own health comes first, and towards that I start with a healthy soil and work upwards. Julius Hensel recognized this truth, for which reason he wrote his little book, *Bread From Stones*, which has gifted me with the title to this chapter.

Julius Hensel was a student of agricultural chemistry, a biochemist and a nutritionist. His book was first published in 1894. It was both a rebuttal to chemical farming as supported by the thesis of Justus von Liebig and the introduction to an alternative method of farming, later styled organic.

It is interesting to compare the careers of Julius Hensel and Justus von Liebig. They were contemporaries, with von Liebig probably a few years ahead of Hensel. Von Liebig was born in 1803 and died in 1873. He was a top chemist, and made the discoveries on which several industries were based, including chemical (N, P and K) agriculture. He found that the ashes which remained from ashed grains consisted mainly of potassium and phosphate. From this he concluded that potassium-phosphate must be restored to the soil, a very one-sided conclusion. Von Liebig had forgotten to take into account the straw, in which only small quantities of phosphoric acid are found because this substance during the process of maturing passes from the stalk

VON LIEBIG'S N-P-K THEORY

The simplistic nitrogen-phosphorus-potassium idea harks back to von Liebig's lectures before the British Association for the Advancement of Science, at which time he made the point that "the primary source whence man and animals derive the means of their growth and support is the vegetable kingdom. Plants, on the other hand, find new nutritive materials only in inorganic substances." Von Liebig translated this to mean that one had only to analyze by an ash test the produce of an acre and "return the nutrients" used to maintain fertility. The end of this line of thinking came in 1843, when von Liebig issued his *mea culpa*:

von Liebig's Mea Culpa

I had sinned against the wisdom of our creator, and received just punishment for it. I wanted to improve his handiwork, and in my blindness, I believed that in this wonderful chain of laws, which ties life to the surface of the earth and always keeps it rejuvenated, there might be a link missing that had to be replaced by me—this weak powerless nothing....

What might justify my actions is the circumstance, that a man is the product of his time, and he is only able to escape the commonly accepted views if a violent pressure urges him to muster all of his strength to struggle free of these chains of error. The opinion, that plants draw their food from a solution that is formed in the soil through rainwater, was everyone's belief. It was engraved into my mind. This opinion was wrong and the source of my foolish behavior.

When a chemist makes mistakes in rating agricultural fertilizers, don't be too critical of his errors, because he has had to base his conclusions upon facts which he can't know from his own experience, but rather, has to take from agricultural texts as true and reliable. After I learned the reason why my fertilizers weren't effective in the proper way, I was like a person that received a new life. For along with that, all processes of tillage were not explained as to their natural laws. Now that this principle is known and clear to all eyes, the only thing that remains is the astonishment of why it hadn't been discovered a long time ago. The human spirit, however, is a strange thing: "Whatever doesn't fit into the given circle of thinking, doesn't exist."

—von Liebig's quotation cited by Charles Walters in Fletcher Sims' Compost

into the grain. If he had calculated the seed, roots and stalks, he could have found what we now know, that in the whole plant there is as much lime and magnesium as potassium and sodium, and that phosphoric acid forms furnish only a tenth part of the sum of these basic nutrients. The chemistry of that day was not sophisticated enough to pick up the trace minerals, and von Liebig completely overlooked these.

At the time, it probably mattered little to him which direction agriculture was taking. He was unaware that his findings would have such an impact. For some time he was just a chemist doing his job. The villains were the chemical industries and the bankers. They seized upon von Liebig's findings to parlay them into a huge industry based upon cartel and monopoly arrangements. They succeeded beyond their fondest dreams. By 1883, "scientific" farming methods were already sickening the soil, the plants, the animals and human beings.

Von Liebig claimed that plants require basically the elements nitrogen, phosphorous and potash. It was on the basis of this conception that chemical fertilizers were manufactured and moved into trade channels. Hensel, on the other hand, claimed that plants need more nutrients than the so-called basic elements. He stressed the importance of trace nutrients. In place of the chemical fertilizers, Hensel recommended minerals found in pulverized rocks, especially granite, a primordial rock which contains the main trace minerals that meet the needs of plant life. Hensel first made his almost serendipitous discovery of powdered rock fertilization when he was a miller. One day, while milling grains, he noticed that some stones were mixed in and ground into a meal. He sprinkled this stone meal over the soil of his garden and was surprised to note how the vegetables took on a new, more vigorous growth. This led him to repeat the experiment by grinding more stones and applying the stone meal to fruit trees. The fruit made a nice improvement. Vegetables also benefitted from stone flour application.

Encouraged by these results, Hensel put his stone meal on the market, and wrote extensively on its superiority over acid treated salt fertilizers. At the same time he opposed the use of raw animal manure, and the nitrogen theory on which it was based. He claimed that when plants are supplied stone meal, plenty of water, air and sunshine, they grow healthy even if the soil is poor in nitrogen. It was his belief that plants took their nitrogen from the air under conditions of stone fertilization.

In opposing the use of chemical fertilizer, Hensel awoke the ire of a powerful enemy which resolved to liquidate him. Unfair competition destroyed Hensel's stone meal business, and his product soon disappeared off the market. His book was literally proscribed. *Bread From Stones*, in which Hensel expounded new and revolutionary theories opposing the doctrines of von Liebig, was out of step with the conventional wisdom of the hour, also ridiculed the "von Liebig meat extract." Hensel was a vegetarian. He soon found *Bread From Stones* suppressed, its publication stonewalled and existing copies removed from libraries. Fortunately, *Bread From Stones* is now kept in print by *Acres U.S.A.*

Hensel claimed that the use of various powdered rocks such as granite, limestone, rock phosphate, etc., in place of salt fertilizers, would lead to permanent restoration of even poor soils to equal the balanced mineral content of the best of virgin soils. The rock powders thus applied, he said would remain year after year and not be washed away by rains or irrigation water. Since foods thus mineralized would be healthy and immune to plant diseases and insect pests, there would be no need for the expense and danger of spraying toxic rescue chemicals.

The next milestone in the history of organic farming was provided by Rudolf Steiner in 1924 in his eight lectures to farmers. Again, as in Hensel's time in 1894, farmers were concerned about the continual degradation of their soils, crops and consequently deteriorating health of animals and man. As related in chapters 4, 5, and 6, Steiner clearly spelled out the roles of silica rocks, the "limes," and the clays.

There is an interesting contradiction in the teachings of the two men, Hensel and Steiner. Hensel was a staunch vegetarian. He had no use for meat. He had no use for animal manure. He claimed fine crushed rock was superior to animal manure. Hensel pointed out the problems with using manure, which are still true if raw manure is spread on the soil. It is hard to believe that he didn't know the difference between raw manure and composted manure, but if he did know the difference, his writings do not reveal this insight. On the other hand, Steiner took the position that true agriculture cannot take place without the use of animal manure. Animals belong to the Earth just as much as man, and they have their contribution to make. Most of Steiner's lectures dealt with composting animal manures. In fact, the very heart of Biodynamics is the preparations complex which goes into the compost pile. I probably should not take sides regarding the difference of opinion of these two men, but I will state unequivocally that the basis of my fertilization program is animal-based compost and rock powders.

Steiner had no more luck than Hensel in convincing the agricultural world that chemical farming leads only to disease and death.

Other prophets of mineral fertilization have come progressively on the scene: Albert Carter Savage, William A. Albrecht, John Hamaker and a group of people under the aegis of *Remineralize The Earth*, led by Joanna Campe. The story is now spreading slowly worldwide. More and more companies are promoting rock powders. *Acres U.S.A.* is in the forefront of this crusade. The movement is picking up speed, but complete victory will not be achieved in our time. The battle between sustainable agriculture and chemical agriculture is as basic as the one between right and wrong, good and evil. Each farmer will have to choose, but at least he or she will know the choices.

In one way or another, I have covered the use of these enlivened rock powders in the soil, and their benefits to crops. I have not said much about their benefits to animals and mankind. While I was a chemist at Brookside Laboratory in the 1960s there were only two rock powders used commercially. One was Planters Soil Conditioner and the other was Micro-Min, now known as Flora-Stim. Both are still being used in production agriculture. While they were promoted as soil conditioners, many farmers were feeding them to their livestock. I worked with Cliff Myer, sales manager for Planters Soil Conditioner, and Ike Falb, sales manager for Micro-Min. Planters is a silicate rock powder rich in sulfur and calcium, whereas MicroMin is a marcasite clay rich in both sulfur and iron. We knew that these rock powders were doing a good job in treating the soil and promoting good nutrition in the livestock, but we scratched our heads in vain searching for the reason.

We would go on the farms where these rock powders were being fed to the animals and invariably the animals would be alert and have glossy coats and shining eyes.

A CASE FOR ENLIVENED ROCK POWDERS

After plastering the walls of a new calf barn, E.R. Kuck noticed that the animals literally ate the plaster off the walls of their stalls. Calves had been scouring at the time. Almost immediately scouring stopped, and Kuck—consulting with William A. Albrecht—determined that the hungry animals were in fact after the calcium carbonate and the magnesium carbonate in the plaster material. These nutrients had been mined out of the soil of the dairy operation and never replaced.

In December 1946, E.R. Kuck issued a report, *Better Crops with Plant Food*, published by the American Potash Institute. The article was picked up by the farm press and given wide distribution. Feedback arrived almost immediately—some one thousand letters from farmers telling of their own problems and asking for help. There were also sixteen letters from academic folk condemning Kuck in vitriolic terms, and denouncing the significance of magnesium in animal nutrition. Moreover, the college people seemed to think that no farmer had the right to make such observations and tell it the way it was without the imprimatur of a credentialed institution.

The sheer desperation of those animals emerged time and time again in William A. Albrecht's writings. "Our dietary essential minerals are taken as organo-inorganic compounds. We are not mineral eaters. Neither are the animals. When any of them take to the mineral box, isn't it an act of desperation?"

>   —*Charles Walters*
>   *in* A Life in the Day of an Editor

What promotes glossy coats? Silica! What promotes shining eyes? Silica! What promotes alertness? Silica! Livestock might be eating enlivened rock powders as a mineral supplement, or they might be eating the crops grown using these rock powders. Either way or both ways, the results were the same.

What are some of these enlivened rock powders fed to farm animals? Every farmer knows about feeding lime sold by almost every lime company. I have already mentioned Planters Soil Conditioner and Flora-Stim. Here are a few others. Details presented here are fleshed out in the GRAMMAR OF THE SUBJECT section of this book.

AZOMITE. This is a hydrated sodium calcium alumino silicate of volcanic origin. It is sold by Peak Minerals of Colorado Springs, Colorado.

DYNA-MIN. Here we have an all natural prehistoric silicate well proved, well documented feed supplement for all classes of livestock. It is sold by Agri-Dynamics, Martins Creek, Pennsylvania, and also by TransNational Agronomy, Grand Rapids, Michigan.

CLOD BUSTER. This trade-named product is a geological mix of humus montmorillonite clay and silicates. It moves into trade channels through Agronics, Inc., Albuquerque, New Mexico.

NUTRICARB, is also a trade-named product, actually bituminous coal. It is sold by Ridzon Farms of New Waterford, Ohio. I well remember that when I worked at Brookside Laboratory, a number of our farmer clients fed coal to their livestock.

There are many enlivened rock powders, all of which are successfully used as feed supplements. I have tried to restrict this exposition to enlivened rock powders that make good feed supplements. The problem is that each state has its own feed registration laws. Most of these laws, sales and regulations make the promotion of rock powders extremely difficult, if not impossible. It is much simpler to sell the rock powders to the farmer. It is his responsibility to use them properly, relying on his own knowledge.

Much the same is true for human beings. If it is difficult to sell the enlivened rock powders as feed supplements for animals, it is impossible to sell them for human consumption. There are several exceptions. The all powerful Food and Drug Administration rules with a heavy, iron-fisted hand. The only way to proceed for those who want to take a rock powder as a supplement is to take the entire responsibility for choosing the rock powder, and instructions for use. What they do with it after they get it is their own business.

There are two exceptions which I know of. Pascalite is a bentonite clay mined in the Big Horn Mountains of Wyoming. It is approved under GRAS (generally regarded as safe) rules. Home base for Pascalite, Inc. is Worland, Wyoming.

The second one is Azomite, which is a montmorillonite clay approved under GRAS. It is mined in an arid desert area of Utah. It travels to market courtesy of Peak Minerals, Colorado Springs, Colorado.

What is good for animals generally is good for *Homo sapiens*. Physiologically, human beings are not that different. The human skin is a vital organ and silica is one of its important elements. Silica promotes strong bones. We have been taught the importance of calcium in our bones, but nothing is said about silica. Silicon is the forgotten element in our bodies. Much the same is true for soils. The strength of bones is more dependent upon silicon than calcium. Calcium may confer bulk on bones, but it is silica which furnishes most of the strength. When the farmer has a problem with his grain lodging, he had better look to silica, which should be in grain stems but is lacking. It is silica that makes for strong grain stems.

Earlier, I mentioned Rudolf Schindele of Austria, one of the discoverers of enlivened rock powders bringing life back into dying trees. He attests to taking two teaspoons of his rock powder daily and his formerly white hair regained some of its youthful color. In chapter 17 of *Secrets of The Soil*, the star of the story is Rollin Anderson, a ninety-three year old man still active and working the mine from which Azomite is extracted. He takes a teaspoon of Azomite each meal. John Hamaker related in his book, *Survival of Civilization*, that he takes from one fourth to one half teaspoon daily. He started taking it to find out if it would relieve his chronic constipation, which it did.

I should probably relate my own experience with taking an enlivened rock powder. I started out taking a quarter teaspoon a day, thinking I would start out on the low side and maybe work higher if I felt some improvement. For several months nothing happened. I felt neither better nor worse. Then I started having a little problem and quit after which I returned to normal. If the animal or the man is already getting enough minerals in his daily food, then taking a rock powder as a supplement is useless. Evidently, I was already getting enough minerals in my daily food and taking the rock powder was overdoing a good thing. Anyone who feeds animals enlivened rock powder, or takes them must realize that in a very real sense he/or she has taken on the role of veterinarian or doctor and should observe closely improvements or upsets.

We have now followed the paramagnetic or enlivened rock powders to their conclusion. The chief purpose of this book has been met, the bottom line has been written and perhaps the book should be concluded. The five chapters which follow are supplemental, and expand on the subject. The reader is invited to read on. The story of the enlivened rock powders can be read in many related places, not the least of which define history, the planet's legacy, and its likely scenarios as we enter Century 21.

13

ANCIENT WISDOM TRANSFORMED

Where did ancient wisdom thrive? It evidently thrived on all continents among all races of people! Among the Egyptians, Mayans, Incas, Asians, Indians, Chinese, among Mound Builders of North America and Aborigines of Australia. Ancient wisdom pervaded the Earth everywhere.

How could we define ancient wisdom? Ancient wisdom was an intuitive wisdom. As a creature of the Divine, man knew many things not from his intellectual mind—because his mind had not yet evolved that far—but as a consequence of communication with the Divine. He might not have been aware of that line of communication, but it was there. This should not be hard to understand. Our animals display this type of wisdom. The migrating birds know exactly where to go, what routes to take, how to navigate and when to start. We enjoy the hummingbirds and in season set up a feeder for them outside the kitchen window so we can watch them. About the middle of May a hummingbird will appear at our kitchen window and cavort around there until we, in a hurry, install the feeder and fill it with sugar water. This little creature is from the same family that was with us the previous year, and knew exactly how to get back to our house. Everyone knows similar stories of dogs or cats or horses or wild animals, each a symbol of memory. They have a wisdom we don't understand because we have lost ours. Yet at one time, for us, it was an ancient wisdom.

The mind of man evolves much as the Earth evolves. The solar system also evolves, and our universe evolves. There seems to be a divine time schedule, and all parts, including man, must evolve in a synchronized manner. In any evolutionary process, there are a few who get left behind.

In ancient times man had an intuitive wisdom, but in his evolution he has had to discard it in order to move on. He had to train his mind and develop an intellectual wisdom. He could no longer look to divinely implanted instinct for his wisdom, but had to develop that rare commodity as one of his own attributes. This should not be hard to understand. Just observe our children. In their early years they look to us for their every need. As they grow older and more knowledgeable, not necessarily wiser, they become less dependent upon us and finally, almost as an act of rebellion, they let us know that they no longer want to be dependent upon us, but are now desirous of fending for themselves. I can well remember the day my dad and I squared off. I was in high school and had gotten vehemently independent on an issue. My dad won the day when he informed me that so long as I put my feet under his table, he was the boss. I did not sit at his table too long after that. That was not bad, it was good. The time had come for me to get out into the world and make it on my own. So it was with ancient man. He had to develop his own wisdom and quit looking to the father figure of mythology.

The transition period between the old intuitive wisdom and the acquisition of the new intellectual wisdom was traumatic. Civilizations fell, including the kingdoms of Egypt and the Mayan culture. The old had to fall away before the new had a chance to start. In Europe this period was termed the Dark Ages. Egypt's ancient civilization was

SACRED LANDSCAPE

New England stone mounds are, for the most part, assumed to have been the work of historical farmers clearing their fields of boulders for cultivation, a view that persists in spite of the fact that similar mounds are found all over America and attributed to aboriginal people. Although New England farm lore includes the use of so-called "manure stones," scattered heaps in a cultivated field built to enrich the soil beneath them, a great number of groups of stone heaps are located on land with no historical record of cultivation and clearly unsuitable for it. Many groups of up to 200 mounds are located on rocky hilltops where cultivation is out of the question. And while we know that isolated stone mounds were used as markers in laying out seventeenth-century town boundaries and were similarly used as property bounds through the nineteenth century, at least some of these were preexisting, and in any case this accounts for only a few. Many mounds were constructed with curbs, walls, pits, cavities, or in curiously regular or irregular shapes suggesting effigies, while others mark astronomical sightlines from stone structures to the horizon.

> —*James W. Mavor, Jr. and Byron E. Dix*
> *in* Manitou, The Sacred Landscape of New England's Native Civilization

torn asunder by successive invasions of the Persians, Greeks, Romans, Arabs and Turks. The library at Alexandria contained an estimated 490,000 volumes of literature from Rome, Greece, India and Egypt. It took only a day or two to destroy this font of knowledge, and centuries to replace it.

Parallel to the fall of the ancient Egyptian civilization was the fall of the Mayan civilization in Central America. It is estimated that the Mayan civilization got underway about B.C. 600, and finally collapsed, A.D. 900. It had flourished for the short life of 1,500 years. The exact cause of the collapse of the Mayan culture has never been determined. It has been postulated that it fell away as a result of internecine wars, droughts, famine and other roads to ruin that civilization always seems to travel.

My wife and I visited the Mayan country in 1992. We hired a bright young Mayan as our guide for a week. He told us that the priests had become corrupt and the people would no longer follow them. If the truth could be known, the line of priests had probably come to an end and those who followed were priests in name only, not in wisdom. The fact remains that this civilization had to fall because it was built upon intuitive wisdom for which the end had come. The Mayan people, as with the Egyptian people, are still living there, but their grand civilization has been blown away, like a leaf in the wind. These civilizations parallel each other in many ways. They were built upon the priesthood class, initiates who could communicate with the divine font of wisdom. When the priesthood class went into decline, the civilization followed.

Both peoples were pyramid builders. The classical Egyptian pyramid is Cheops, also known as the Great Pyramid of Giza. It covers thirteen acres, has more than two and a half million blocks of limestone and granite, each block weighing from two to seventy tons and rising to a height of four hundred eighty feet, which is about the height of a modern forty story building. No one knows for sure when it was built, but one date, B.C. 2644, has been accepted by many Egyptologists. That was a longer time span between its construction up to the birth of Christ than after the crucifixion to the present. For man, that is one long time. This pyramid has held great fascination for me ever since I visited it in 1984 with the *Acres U.S.A.* tour group. We entered the King's Chamber where we joined Phil Callahan in some ancient chants. Several mornings later most of the men in our party , and two women, climbed to the peak in time to see the Sun rise over the desert. I well remember while climbing at about the halfway mark looking over my shoulder at the ground far below. It was a dizzying experience and I never looked at the ground again until I reached the top.

Why was the pyramid built? There are several answers and all of them are undoubtedly right. Peter Tompkins, writing in *Secrets of the Great Pyramids*, stressed the structure as a giant observatory from which the astronomers of that day could calculate the dimensions of the Earth, its distance from the Sun, the length of the year, the passage of the stars and many other astronomical observations. The Hardys and Killicks in their book, *Pyramid Energy: The Philosophy of God, The Science of Man*, claim the pyramid was built to maintain a harmonic balance between this world and the solar system. It was built in the exact center of the land area of the Earth. Phil Callahan, in *Ancient Mysteries, Modern Vision*, states his thesis that the pyramid is a huge paramagnetic antennae capable of focusing like a lens waves of paramagnetism into a tower, the King's Chamber. The pyramid serves many functions. Do not modern churches serve in many capacities? Perhaps one function was as an induction site for high initiates. It is claimed that Moses, Plato and Pythagoras were initiated at that sight, as were many other great initiates. Alexander the Great meditated there, as did Napoleon Bonaparte. Both men had key roles to play in the course of western civilization.

The question has no doubt suggested itself—why am I going into such detail about the pyramids?

The pyramids are collectors and broadcasters of paramagnetic energy. Egypt has nearly one hundred pyramids located in a stretch of seventy miles. Conceptualize, if you can, the enormity of the paramagnetic energy enveloping that section of Egypt. Then reflect on the connection, if any, with the Mayan country in Central America.

This is another country dotted with many pyramids. I have never heard a number quoted, but I would guess there are thirty-five to forty, a few of which may not even have been discovered yet. They are not as large as the Egyptian pyramids. They rarely rise to a height of one hundred fifty feet. With several exceptions, these pyramids take on a little different shape from that of their Egyptian counterparts. These pyramids have the broad bases and sloping faces, but they do not rise to a peak. For some, the sloping faces give way to a parapet structure near the top. For others, the sloping faces merge into several small rectangular rooms at the top. Regardless of the final configuration at the summit, they always have a structure designed for astronomical purposes. The ancient Mayans were great astronomers, probably on a par with their Egyptian counterparts. They were the world's best calendar makers of all time. Their calendars extended both back into history and forward to world events yet to take place. Their basic calendar covers five great world periods. We are presently in the fifth. Each world period ends in a cataclysmic disaster. The first two world periods ended in disasters difficult for us to understand. Later, the disasters became well understood. The third world period was ended by fire. The fourth period was terminated by the great flood. The fifth period—the one in which we find ourselves—will end in cataclysmic earthquakes. That is scheduled to happen in A.D. 2011. Maybe that will be the one we refer to as the "big one."

More to the point of this book, these Mayan pyramids, as with their Egyptian counterparts, were constructed mostly of limestone, a highly energized rock. The Mayans must have known that the orientation of their pyramids affected the entire country with their paramagnetic forces. This was a part of their ancient wisdom.

The pyramids were the key structures in ancient Egypt, but the Egyptians also developed the use of obelisks. Basically, obelisks were sundials by use of which further astronomical measurements could be made. Unlike the pyramids, which were built of limestone, the obelisks were cut from quartz. The *Acres U.S.A.* group viewed the quarry from which most of the obelisks were cut. That quarry yielded a very pretty red quartz sprinkled with black spots. Quartz is a silica rock, polaric to limestone, and highly paramagnetic. So that is yet another factor in the paramagnetism permeating Egypt.

The Mayans did not have obelisks like the Egyptians, but they had steles. A stele is a standing stone reminiscent of some of our grave markers, albeit much larger. They stand six to eight feet tall, three to four feet per side, and measure three to four inches in thickness. The tops are rounded. They are inscribed with Mayan glyphs memorializing one of their kings or high priests. Many other peoples throughout the world utilized standing stones. Probably the most enigmatic standing stones in the world are those of Easter Island. They stand about fifteen feet high, weigh close to thirty tons, and were carved from volcanic rock. Volcanic rock is nearly always paramagnetic, basalt being a good example. The people who constructed those standing stones did so based on intuitive wisdom.

The Irish round towers of which Phil Callahan has ably written are structures manifesting ancient wisdom in at least two different ways. They were built as astronomical observatories and had the dual function of collecting and broadcasting paramagnetic forces. We have considered Egypt with its maze of pyramids and obelisks, and the Mayan country with its maze of pyramids and steles. Now we can add Ireland with its sixty odd round towers.

To this impressive list of structures, that collect and broadcast paramagnetic forces, we must add North America with its stone circles and earthen mounds. These structures were not built by the Indians of the near colonial era, but by prehistoric races. The Indians would be their descendants, as the present Mayan people are the descendants of the Mayan pyramid builders. I know of one archeological dig in Ohio for which the ancient people were dated approximately 7,000 to 8,000 years ago. These structures appear to have taken their design from an intuitive wisdom, now lost for all time.

Pyramids, obelisks, steles, round towers, stone circles and earthen works all hold in escrow secrets vastly more recondite than the formulas for putting a man on the Moon. The form of each structure is vital to its effectiveness. Go into the old section of any old cemetery where large monuments are common. Many of them are obelisks, they radiate paramagnetic forces. Maybe right next to an obelisk, cut out of the same kind of rock, will be a huge rectangular stone, highly polished and very attractive, but as far as forces are concerned, it is dead. There are lots of steles and they, too, radiate paramagnetic forces; thus we discover that ancient people involved intuitive wisdom in discerning which form worked.

Indeed, our intuitive wisdom has faded, and selectively it has been replaced by an intellectual wisdom. With our telescopes we can go far beyond prehistoric man in our study of the stars. Can we go further than prehistoric man in developing truly fertile soils? So far we have failed. If anything, we are faltering badly.

Prehistoric man knew how to maintain the forces in his soil. Today we do not even know that soils are supposed to have forces. Only a few are learning quickly that the soil is supposed to have forces and that through our intellect we can devise ways of imparting the necessary forces to the soil. One thing is certain; we will not be building pyramids, obelisks or round towers to do the job.

I make this observation with the science of the day in mind. Sir Isaac Newton (1642-1727), more than any other man, ushered in the scientific era and conferred on mankind an intellectual wisdom on which it is established. It is the conceit of intellectual wisdom that by its very nature it cannot admit to being a part of intuitive wisdom. Science cannot admit intuitive knowledge because knowledge so gained has no standing in a world that depends on precisely measured results carried out in replicated experiments.

This science dogma has its problems, as expressed by William A. Albrecht. "First," he said, "you have to have a vision." In fact, the foundation for most science is entirely a product of vision, as Albert Einstein clearly illustrated when he announced $E=MC^2$. Such a finding could never have been arrived at as a product of experimentation. Much the same is true of Steiner's insight regarding the energy bounce from planet to Sun to silica on spaceship Earth.

To illustrate these several points, it must be stated that science has done very little with magnetism because its practitioners do not understand it. A professor friend of mine once remarked that he did not dare to discuss it in his classroom. To do so would put his professional standing in jeopardy.

Magnetism has been so little investigated that up to twenty-five years ago, Albert Roy Davis and Walter Rawls were able to discover that north pole magnetism was different from south pole magnetism, and of course they suggested ways in which we could take advantage of the difference. Yet the scientific system suggests such a ridiculous attitude on the part of scientists is almost unthinkable.

Using our relatively new found intellectual wisdom, what can we do to reestablish or improve paramagnetism in our soils? By now we know we can do a fair job of restoring a little paramagnetism with the judicious application of rock powders, but this is neither the best solution nor the ultimate one. It is like taking vitamin pills to supplement foods which are lacking in the essential vitamins. If we raise our foods correctly and prepare them correctly, they should contain all of the vitamins we require. If we would incorporate a few practices into our gardening and farming systems, we could establish paramagnetism in soils which indirectly serve us very well.

What are some of the methods we can use? In Ohio we have hundreds of earthworks put up by prehistoric man. There is no way we are going to put up earthworks, but how about raised beds? Nearly every gardener has heard about raised beds and almost all understand that raised beds outperform ordinary beds. The counterpart in farming is "ridge planting."

Donald Schriefer has an entire chapter in his book, *From The Soil Up*, on ridge planting, which is recommended reading for those interested in reestablishing or strengthening soil paramagnetism. In his opening paragraph, he brings out the fact that the Chinese used this system 3,000 years ago—intuitive wisdom again. My observation is, *use your intellectual wisdom and get with it!* Schriefer also brings out the fact that this practice encourages the circulation of soil moisture. As soil moisture circulates so does the soil air and warmth. These are properties of good paramagnetic soil.

For some reason raised beds call into play paramagnetic forces. Rudolf Steiner has something to say about this. "Whenever you have a normal level of soil, whatever is raised above this normal level will show a special tendency to life—a tendency to permeate itself with ethereal vitality." He goes on to say that this is an excellent way in which to raise the organic matter content in a soil. "Hence, you will find it easier to permeate ordinary inorganic mineral earth with fruitful humus substance, or with any waste product in process of decomposition. You will find it easier to do this efficiently if you erect mounds of earth and permeate these with the organic wastes. For then the organic wastes will tend to become inwardly alive—akin to the plant nature."

From an intellectual viewpoint, we still do not totally understand why these raised beds attract paramagnetic forces, or in Steiner's words, *the etheric forces*. If we wanted to bring Wilhelm Reich into the picture, we could call these forces orgone energy. These forces are "living forces" and these are the forces we want in our soils and our food crops.

From time to time someone asks me how I would construct a small round tower. Nature has already answered that question for us with trees. It is a crime against nature to cut down all trees, as in clear cutting forest or clear cutting a farm acreage. Nature takes her revenge in several ways. First, there is a loss of paramagnetism, and in extreme cases there is a salt buildup. In 1988 I was with the *Acres U.S.A.* group which visited Australia and New Zealand. Sheep farming is the big thing in many parts of Australia.

Sheep ranchers had cut down all of their trees. Often one could see to the horizons without a tree in sight. Station managers wanted every square foot of land available for grazing. As a consequence, much of the land has developed salt areas, and nothing grows in a salt soil very well. Australia has people who know the answer. After all, Australia is the home of permaculture.

Permaculture has spread to the United States, where the art is alive and well. One of the Australian permaculture practitioners told me that as few as three trees per acre would prevent salt buildup in the soil. This was hard to believe, but Leland Taylor has confirmed for me numerous instances where salt buildup was checked and reversed with the application of Clod Buster, a marine deposit humate product. This is hard to believe. Yet these two claims lead me to believe that as paramagnetism is restored, salt buildups reverse themselves.

Rudolf Schindele revitalized his forest trees with the application of a paramagnetic silica rock powder. For people who want to construct a small round tower, perhaps an arbor day spirit with a heavy application of a paramagnetic silica rock powder from trunk to drip line would be a substitute. This treatment for ten trees would equal ten round towers, all of them with nature on their side.

Another way to utilize a tree as a round tower is to place a stone circle around it. In so doing, you'll be upgrading the intuitive wisdom of prehistoric man. We know that there have been and still are many prehistoric stone circles in North America. They invite into the area strong paramagnetic forces. I don't know how they do it, but they do it. You may take a group of stones lying around and find they exhibit no paramagnetic force whatsoever. Rearrange those stones into a stone circle and you have performed a miracle. That stone circle now collects and broadcasts paramagnetic forces. After several weeks in this circle, each stone takes on a permanent paramagnetism which will manifest even if the stone is removed from the circle.

J.I. Rodale, founder of the popular magazine, *Organic Gardening*, observed that stone mulching was highly effective in gardening. He edited and published the book, *Stone Mulching in the Garden* in 1949. Actually, the book is a collection of anecdotes from many people on how stone mulching improved their gardens and trees. However, stone mulching of trees was the focal point of the book. There were photographs in *Stone Mulching*, and from this evidence the reader discerned that stone mulchers unwittingly created stone circles. One chapter in the Rodale book explains why stone mulching works.

1. The stone mulch does away with the need to plow or disc, leaving microlife under the stones undisturbed. In turn, microlife flourishes under the stones.

2. Stone mulching conserves water.

3. It causes the soil to be well aerated.

4. The practice creates a temperature regulation system beneficial to both the soil and microlife living in it.

5. Stones often crumble, furnishing valuable minerals.

Do you recognize this inventory of observations as paramagnetic effects? Secondly, the growers who were stone mulching their trees and gardens were tapping into paramagnetism.

We have all seen herb and flower gardens laid out in artistic circles with stones interlaced as part of the design. Invariably these gardens produced vigorous herbs, flowers and shrubs.

How does one make a stone circle? Almost any stones will work—hard stones, soft stones, round stones, flat stones, stones of all sizes. There is no limit to the size of stones which can be used. I generally like to use stones from approximately five pounds up to as heavy as I can lift without undue effort. My wife will take smaller stones about the size of a double fist and place them around her little herb gardens. Arbitrarily, I use about eight stones, placing them at the cardinal points of the compass. I feel that somehow the stone circle is tied in with the magnetic grid of the Earth. Your ideas on stone circles may be as good as mine, so use your own judgment.

There is one drawback to stone circles. You can hardly use them in areas which require mowing. There was a time when I had a lot of stone circles around my orchard trees. They were fine for the trees but I couldn't mow around the trees. An orchard must be mowed at least once or maybe twice a season, or brambles, weed trees and other undesirable weeds will infest the grove. I have retained a few stone circles in my orchard and I feel that they may have an effect almost as much as a larger number.

In ancient America the natives had their medicine wheels, which were stone circles dedicated to a higher purposes. The Seneca Indians have a legend applicable for old and young alike but, especially, the children.

I am a member of the Stone Family
We have sustained the balance for our Mother Earth
And supported all life from the dawn of birth

And help them find their inner sight

I am the lightsound that flows throughout the Earth
Bestowing sacred gifts upon all things at birth
My lightsound travels with a silent call
To link all things as one and each one as all

Come to me my little friends
Where sacred life never ends
Youth walks closer to Mother Earth
Sensing her rhythm and inner worth

Honor this life seven fold
Earn the wisdom endless told
Stones hold the wisdom of countless ages
And pass on the peace of ancient sages

So far I have discussed a few things anyone can do to promote paramagnetic forces in his soil. To further plumb earthly forces, one must be a dowser. There is no other way. The Earth is a living organism. The Earth has nerves even as we have nerves, but we refer to them as energy lines. The Earth has a master grid of energy lines which break down into smaller and smaller subdivisions so that there are literally millions of energy lines crisscrossing the face of the planet. Approximately half of the lines run north-south in conformity with the magnetic lines of the Earth. The other half run East-West. Steiner tells us that there is an earthly energy which runs from East to West even as the Sun travels from East to West. This energy is directly related to the Sun's movement and ceases when the Sun sets and starts up again when the Sun rises. There are a few diagonal energy lines, but they are fewer in number. Where the energy lines inter-

MAGNETISM

According to ancient legends a shepherd named Magnes was tending his flocks. It is told that his staff made of iron was pulled by an unseen force toward a large rock where it was held and resisted the boy's efforts to free it from the surface of the rock. This rock mineral became known as The Magnes Stone. Today we call this magnetic natural material lodestone. From the young shepherd's name, Magnes, we have magnet and magnetism—an unseen, untouchable energy that is the basis for the development of electricity as we know it today that furnishes the power for our lights, radios and television sets.

Since that time in ancient history scientists have probed this invisible force of nature that produced the first magnet, *lodestone.*

To show the length of time this study and its legends have been known to man let us quote the following: "A.D. 597, St. Augustine came to Britain at the insistence of Pope Gregory I and as he viewed the magnets attracting one to the other and when they were reversed, the magnets opposed each other, with no hand touching either magnet, he stated out loud, 'When I first saw it I was thunderstruck.'"

The magnetism of the shepherd Magnes has presented a great scientific question over many past and present centuries. To this day the true nature of magnetism is still far from being understood. Outstanding space researchers and world-renowned scientists are not applying the true nature and understanding that this important science has for application not only for magnetism itself but also for the application in the other sciences known to man.

Lodestone is magnetic iron ore or iron mineral ore; it is in part the composition of the lava, the molten hot flowing lava of a volcano. As this hot lava flows up, then down the sides of a volcano, it slowly cools, and as it cools the earth's magnetism, the magnetic fields that flow from one pole of the earth to the other pole, passes through the lava and impresses on the lava these fields of magnetism. When the molten lava is cold it has accepted, stored and has in itself that amount of energy that existed on the earth at the time the mineral rock was formed.

—*Albert Roy Davis and Walter C. Rawls, Jr.*
in Magnetism and Its Effects on the Living System

sect or apparently intersect, there may be an energy center, but not in every instance. These energy centers can be likened to acupuncture points.

We all know that it would be ideal to be able to capture the Earth's energy and do away with gasoline, power plants, and other pollution producers. Trees and plants capture some of this solar energy, but not all of growth energy comes from the Sun via the agency of photosynthesis. To strengthen this energy system involving energy lines and energy centers, we first have to find them, and this is done by dowsing. Some energy lines are paramagnetic and some are diamagnetic. Some are alternately para-diamagnetic. The same is true of energy centers. On my paramagnetic energy centers I will have a small pile of paramagnetic silica rocks, a little pyramid, if you please. It is just a neat pile of stones coming to a crest, but with no special dimensions or angles or volume. The volume would be roughly a bushel, but this is just arbitrary, even subjective. Your guess could be as good as mine. On my diamagnetic energy centers I have a small neat pile of limestone and on my para-diamagnetic energy centers I have a bag of para-diamagnetic clay.

Does it work? It certainly does. When I first started working with paramagnetic devices in 1984, there were three energy centers on my little farm. That figure has now grown to twenty-one. All of the soil has a balanced form of paramagnetism.

One additional factor gives a paramagnetism assist in my soil. I build my Biodynamic compost piles on diamagnetic energy centers. The energy from those piles travels along the energy lines to all parts of the farm. This energy works all day, every day. I further explain this concept in the last chapter of this book.

For now, let me quote Martin Brennan, who wrote the

following for the American Society of Dowsers. "While we are born in the shadow of these ancient sites, we still fail to understand them. They stand silently in testimony of something we fail to comprehend. We will only grasp their meaning when we realize the meaning of our own life more fully and that of the living forces around us. To understand the works of enlightened people, we must to a certain extent be enlightened ourselves. Those who refuse to see a higher consciousness than our own in the works of Megalithic Man see only graves and forts and reflect their own mentality and not that of Megalithic Man. Those who see the vision of unity expressed in the stones will not only see a reality that has sustained man on this planet for thousands of years, but will also see a vision of the future—a way of reconciliation with the totality of Nature and our place in it—and perhaps the only way we can achieve harmony and survival with it."

STONEHENGE

From the last important Stonehenge book in Latin comes the modern spelling of the name for that great stone circle, and from Samuel Daniel's lament we harvest a refreshing view of the ignorance "unsparing time forces on us."

The Ignorance, with fabulous discourse,
  Robbing faire Arte and Cunning of their right,
  Tels, how those stones, were by the Deuils force,
  From *Affrike* brought to *Ireland* in a night,
  And thence, to Britannie, by *Magicke* course,
  From Gyants hands reedem'd, by Merlins sleight...
  With this old Legend then Credulitie
  Holdes her content, and closes vp her care:
But is Antiquitie so great a liar?

14

RADIONIC AMPLIFICATION OF PARAMAGNETIC FORCES

If any of the foregoing lessons have reached their mark, the reader-farmer will want to reestablish or strengthen the paramagnetic forces in soils. How to accomplish this goal may still be open to questions. Several methods have been discussed available:

1. Apply a paramagnetic rock powder.
2. Create raised beds or ridge tilling.
3. Utilize the Earth's energy centers.
4. Work with trees as energy towers.

We might be able to add a fifth possibility, namely utilization of radionics to speed up the several processes. Before I go into any details, I want those interested in this approach to understand a few caveats.

1. The procedure at this time is strictly experimental. It has worked for me and a friend of mine. The limited experience precludes my saying that it will work for you, but it should.

2. For this reason it should be tried only by those who already have a radionic unit and would enjoy the experimentation involved.

3. Any radionic unit should be capable of amplifying and broadcasting paramagnetic forces. I used the simplest unit available—a beam projector.

4. Since the procedure involves only amplification and

RADIONICS

The position of radionics in the spectrum has been identified and noted in Phil Callahan's *Exploring the Spectrum.*

Radionics is simply a low level energy system that can be directed. Dr. Pat Flanagan once explained the concept in an *Acres U.S.A.* interview.

"When an operator's mind and emanations from the tuner are on the same wavelength, a type of resonance is established, and the detector indicates this mode. The Hieronymus detector is simply a sheet of bakelite or plexiglass under which is placed a flat spirally wound coil, connected to the output of the amplifier and the ground. When resonance is established, there is a change of tactile characteristic in the detector. The change of characteristic is detected by lightly running the fingertips on the surface of the detector plate while tuning the vernier dial of the prism. Galen Hieronymus established numbers which correlated with the known chemical elements and combinations.... Although the Hieronymus machine cannot be explained by modern physics, it does have merit by the fact that the results can be duplicated."

broadcasting, no operator involvement is required.

Those who work with the soil should realize that lime does not go to work immediately after application but requires time to "digest." The same would be true of the other paramagnetic rock powders. Let us recall the definition of paramagnetism as the ability to resonate to the magnetic fields of the cosmos. Since that is a phenomenon exhibited by a paramagnetic rock powder, it ought to resonate to a similar electromagnetic force emitted by a radionics unit. And this, of course, is the "theory" of the radionic unit. If I have spread some basalt on my garden and I want to use a radionic unit to broadcast the requisite electromagnetic force, what am I going to put into the well of my radionic unit? Basalt, of course. The radionic unit will amplify and broadcast the force of the basalt. I will leave it to others to define the exact position in the spectrum this phenomenon takes place. The basalt I have applied to my garden soil will resonate to that force.

There are a few principles everyone working with paramagnetic forces should understand. When working with enlivened rock powders we are working with vortex forces. Consider the vortex pattern of a tornado or hurricane. The vortex pattern of the silica rock powders is counter-clockwise, moving in an upward spiral . The vortex pattern of the "lime" rock powders is clockwise, moving in a downward spiral.

For the beam projector to broadcast these forces, synchronism must be achieved. The beam projector has a well with a coil of wire wrapped around it. If the beam projector is to be used to broadcast a silica rock powder force, the wire must be wound in a counter-clockwise position. To broadcast the force "lime" powder, the wire must be wound in a clockwise direction. This entails two projectors,

LOW-LEVEL ENERGY

A French scientist, namely Jacques Arsene d'Arsonval of the Paris *Academie des Sciences*, wrote voluminously about these wave connections, and a Russian engineer named Georges Lakhovsky set down many of the principles Phil Callahan was later to refine as proof of insect and plant communication in the infrared. Lakhovsky spelled it out in a little work entitled, *The Secret of Life*. What Lakhovsky said was transparently clear in its implications. He compared the nucleus of a living cell to an electrical oscillating circuit. The nucleus of that cell was made up of tubular filaments, chromosomes and the mitochondria. It had insulating material and was filled with a fluid containing all the mineral salts in sea water. This fluid conducted electricity. He compared the filaments in that cell to oscillating circuits capable of oscillating according to a specific frequency. The rationale for some parts of this low level energy was stated in *Acres U.S.A.* as follows:

"Our bodies contain approximately 200 quintillion cells. In this fabulous number there are hardly two cells vibrating with the same frequency, this being partly due to the incessant activity taking place within the cells, and partly to the specific characteristics of different tissues, plus other factors. Moreover, from a biological point of view, it would be impossible to find at any given time two individual cells exactly alike in every respect. Every cell of every individual tissue of any particular species—plant, animal or man—is characterized by its own oscillatory shock. In disequilibriated cells, it would be necessary to generate as many wavelengths as there are different cells in any given body. The problem would thus seem to be insoluble. With remarkable imaginative insight Lakhovsky finally evolved a solution. He designed a new type of radio-electrical apparatus, the multiple wave oscillator, generating a field in which every cell could find its own frequency and vibrate in resonance. The practical results he obtained in various hospitals soon confirmed the validity of this theory. His agricultural experiments were equally impressive."

> —*Abstracted from* The Secret of Life, *by*
> *Georges Lakhovsky, and extracted from* Acres
> U.S.A. *as quoted*

or the operator can rewind the coil to fit the need. I have three projectors but from time to time I would rewind a coil, which is easy to do. I rewind them by hand taking about fifty turns.

The beam projector will treat about one acre at a time, and it will take about four or five days for a soil in good condition, longer for a soil in poor condition. The only way I know to tell if the soil has been balanced is to dowse for it. My beam projectors were custom made to operate from a twelve volt deep charge marine battery so that I could take them out into the field. The charge would hold only for about two days so I used two batteries, alternating them.

A precautionary note. Some radionic units broadcast from the "stickplate" and not the well. You will have to dowse for this. If this is the case, the windings in the "stickplate" will have to be adjusted accordingly. Silica rock powders broadcast in an upward spiral and will have to be placed under the unit. "Lime" rock powders broadcast in a downward spiral and are placed on top of the "stickplate."

The whole procedure can be complex for those with little knowledge of electronics and is not recommended unless a course of study is completed. But there are individuals who enjoy working with radionics and for them this chapter should get them off to a good start. Sandy Asbill, Route 1, Box 1843, Tiger, Georgia, 30576, can custom-make a very simple beam projector at a low cost.

15

NEUTRALIZING NOXIOUS FORCES

The modern age has brought many benefits to mankind but with the benefits have come hazards. Unfortunately, some of the hazards are not known to most of the people. In many instances big business and big government will not recognize the hazards. Consequently, neither will tell the people about them. Thus it behooves the individual to take whatever precautionary measures are available. Everyone should realize that his or her health is a personal responsibility and cannot be delegated to others.

A good starting point would be the TV set. I realize that TV sets give off extremely short rays which may be injurious to human health, but we have always taken precautionary measures to avoid or at least to minimize those noxious rays. I can pick up those rays with my dowsing instruments at a distance of ten to twelve feet. I used to sit back to stay out of range. Then one day we had a visitor, Dale Johns, from Boulder, Colorado. He had a lot of interest in paramagnetic rock powders. His interest was mostly Azomite, so he suggested that we place a jar of Azomite on the TV set to see what might happen. Nothing happened. I knew that the forces of paramagnetic silica rock powders travelled in an upward spiral and perhaps a jar of Azomite should be placed underneath the TV set. Eureka! That canceled out the noxious rays to within a foot of the TV set. Now, we could sit closer to the TV set if we wished. We then tried other paramagnetic silica rock powders, and they all worked.

The paramagnetic lime rock powders give off forces travelling in a downward spiral, so perhaps if a jar of lime was placed on top of the TV set, the same reduction of noxious rays would occur. We tried it and it worked. The forces from these paramagnetic rock powders interfere somehow with the rays coming out of the TV set, for all practical purposes, canceling them out.

From TV sets my thoughts turned to microwave ovens. The manufacturers claim that their ovens are well guarded and no noxious rays escape. My dowsing picked up stronger noxious rays than those put out by the TV sets. Using the same techniques with the paramagnetic rock powders used with the TV sets, I was able to achieve similar results with microwave ovens. There was one important exception: the noxious rays being stronger to start with, the cancellation was only to about four feet from the ovens. To set the record straight, I checked only several ovens, so I can't claim the same results would be valid for all ovens. As stated previously, the health of each individual is his or her own responsibility, so those concerned individuals will have to do their own checking.

I have no personal experience with computers, but I do understand that some computer operators who sit in front of a computer terminal all day suffer stress symptoms. It is suggested that they try the same technique with paramagnetic rock powders as suggested for TV sets. No harm can occur and perhaps some good will come from it.

Another source of noxious forces are those coming from high power lines. There has been some publicity on this subject, therefore most people have heard of the potential hazards. Several years ago we attended the fiftieth wedding

THE ELF FACTOR

It is now generally known that electromagnetic fields are generated by electrical devices that have become a benchmark for our civilization. Health risks that are a consequence of this pollution form have been ignored and denied, even by the White House, even though the Environmental Protection Agency has proposed that electromagnetic fields be labeled a "Class B carcinogen," much like cigarette smoke.

The coverup might have succeeded except for scientist Robert Becker, an expert in bioelectricity. Dr. Becker's seminal work is *The Body Electric*. In it he detailed the mechanisms by which electric current promotes mitosis, meaning the current cause of cell reproduction. Early in his experiments he discerned that electromagnetic fields could also promote malignant cell growth.

Becker put his findings in perspective with one whiplash line. "Accelerated mitosis is a hallmark of malignancy as well as healing, and long term exposure to extremely low-frequency (ELF) electromagnetic fields has been linked to increased rates of cancer in humans."

anniversary of two of our friends. The reception was held in their daughter's home which was off to the side of a high power line. It was a happy occasion and I wasn't about to mention such an unpleasant subject, but on a later occasion brought the hazard to their attention. Being concerned, they asked me what I could recommend. Their house was rectangular and had a basement. I recommended that they place a jar of paramagnetic silica rock powder at the four corners of their basement. They effectively canceled out the radiations from those power lines.

In an earlier chapter I wrote a little about Earth energy lines, most of which are beneficial to us. But there are a relatively few of those lines whose forces are deleterious. They are beneficial to the Earth but are noxious to us. It is theorized that noxious forces originate deep within the Earth as a result of certain types of pressure stresses. If one of these lines passes through a house, the inhabitants may feel a stress. It seems that a person in sleep is more susceptible to this kind of stress and may develop cancer as a result. I personally knew two people who contracted cancer in this manner and died as a result. The noxious lines crossing their beds were found too late. There are several methods for canceling out these noxious forces passing through a house. One method is the same as related for canceling out the forces from high power lines. Place jars of paramagnetic silica powders at the corner of the basement. If there is no basement, the same results can be obtained by placing the jars at the corners of the foundation.

There is an atomic power plant about forty miles from where we live. I have never been concerned about its safety but, on the other hand, I was curious about it. Did it put out atomic radiation? If so, how far did it extend? I drove over one Sunday afternoon when there would be little activity.

When I got within a few miles, I stopped the car, got out and dowsed for any forces which might be emanating from the plant. I got none. I repeated this procedure until I got about a mile from the plant, where I first started picking up some forces. I then drove to its parking lot which was outside of the secured area so I was sure I wasn't trespassing. I repeated my little experiment. This time I sprinkled some paramagnetic silica rock powder on the ground and stood on it when I did my dowsing. I got nothing but as soon as I walked to another area I again picked up the plant's forces. Were the forces I was picking up atomic radiations? I doubt it. Certainly, their safeguards would prevent that, but I was picking up something—possibly some more subtle forces. I honestly don't know what conclusions I can draw from this little experiment other than that our enlivened rock powders can protect us in many situations.

There are gadgets which can be purchased and worn on the body to protect from noxious forces—it is claimed! These claims are partially true. Take the gadget apart and what do you find—a paramagnetic rock powder. If you want to take advantage of this possibility, make your own gadget and save your money.

I know that I have not explored all the possibilities of these enlivened rock powders. They are magic. Use your imagination and you can likely come up with yet another use.

A NEW WAY OF THINKING

Biodynamic agriculture, rather than theorizing, proceeds from what is known. It is known that there is a plant kingdom and an animal kingdom. Their functions are different and complementary. Plants are formative. They build. Animals are transformative, and they recycle or break down and rebuild.

Conventional scientists are apt to say, "Plants build through photosynthesis."

This is all right since plants do photosynthesize. But the BD practitioner is likely to take exception to the implication that photosynthesis is all that is involved in the plant's building. Far from being all, it is only one of the many features of how plants build. It is sloppy thinking to suggest otherwise.

Biodynamic practitioners are likely to talk about formative forces, digestive impulses, cosmic and earthly influences as generalities that they know exist in the broader scheme of things. Though they may know numerous details, they do not want to lose sight of the larger picture. It is better to refrain from citing details as though these are all that exist. This puzzles and annoys people who are so immersed in details that they form snap conclusions, incomplete theories and mistaken assumptions.

—Hugh Lovel in
A Biodynamic Farm, *1994*

16

BIODYNAMIC FORCES

Since this book is about the cosmic forces which are found in enlivened rock powders and how these forces can be put to work in a constructive manner, it seems appropriate to note how some other natural materials with cosmic forces can be utilized to benefit both Earth and mankind. Biodynamic agriculture was introduced by Rudolf Steiner in 1924. There are many aspects to Biodynamic agriculture, nearly all of them dealing with the relationship of the spiritual world with the material world as they affect agriculture. The two worlds are not separate worlds, but parts of the same world.

Although there are many aspects to Biodynamic agriculture, I am going to deal with just two of them. Cosmic forces are involved. We can put these to good use along with the cosmic forces found in enlivened rock powders. The planets Mars, Jupiter and Saturn lend their influences to the Sun which rays them to Earth for the benefit of paramagnetic rock powders. The planets Moon, Venus and Mercury lend their influences to the Sun, which rays them to the Earth for the benefit of diamagnetic rock powders. The mineral kingdom represented by enlivened rock powders plays a key role in this transfer of cosmic forces.

Biodynamic agriculture utilizes the mineral kingdom with a quartz preparation designated as BD 501. The plant and animal kingdoms are the ones principally utilized in bringing these cosmic forces to Earth for utilization in agriculture. There are members of the plant kingdom which have strong connections with individual planets. If we could go back far enough to the birth of the solar system, we could pick up these connections. The easiest connection to make would be between stinging nettle and the Sun. Have you ever inadvertently walked through a patch of stinging nettle and come out with your legs itching and burning? Some of the happiest moments of my life were spent with children leading them on nature walks. I suppose I was a little mean. I would lead them through a stinging nettle patch, not through a heavy infestation, but one that would provide a few itches. I wanted them to learn about stinging nettle and I thought that was the best way. The stems of a stinging nettle plant have thousands of minute silica needles containing minute amounts of formic acid, the same acid that puts the sting in an ant bite. The stinging nettle has silica needles, and silica is one of the Sun elements.

In the same way certain plants have strong affinity to individual planets, so some animal organs have strong attachment to individual planets. The skull, with its hard calcium casement, has a strong connection with the Moon. In the mineral kingdom it is the lime which brings in Moon forces. In the animal kingdom it is the skull. To keep the record straight, I should add that water is technically a mineral and as a mineral also brings in Moon forces. All of this is very confusing since there are many different forces coming from the Moon. Man has not yet reached the stage where he can separate these different forces.

The best way to utilize most of these forces now commands our attention. Composting is one answer to this complicated problem. Composting is more an art than a science. If composting were entirely a science, it would have to be well understood and the resulting product would have to be capable of duplication year after year governed by well laid out principles. There is no way this can be done, since nature does not give us the same materials in the same condition year after year.

Biodynamic agriculture differs from organic agriculture in that it introduces cosmic forces into the art. Otherwise biodynamics follow most of the principles of organic agriculture. In Biodynamic compost we have representative materials from the mineral kingdom (enlivened rock powders), from the plant kingdom (plant residues), from the animal kingdom (animal manures), and forces from the celestial bodies of the solar system. We do not include the planets, Uranus, Neptune and Pluto since they are not "blood related" members of our solar system.

How do we "invoke" the forces from the celestial bodies of the solar system? There are preparations, one for each body, which go into the compost pile. An individual preparation acts as a chemical conduit, channeling in the forces from its planet. An easy way to think of a preparation is to think of a radio tuned in to a particular planet, Venus for example. The radio picks up the waves from Venus, converts them to music and the music penetrates the entire compost pile.

If a person composts according to the Biodynamic principles, there will be not only material values, but spiritual values as well. Accordingly, the food we eat should nourish physically and spiritually. The chief reason for the moral degeneration of so many of our people is the quality of the food they eat. There are no spiritual qualities left in most of our food.

Even as far back as the early 1920s, farmers could see their soils, crops and their livestock degenerating. They asked Rudolf Steiner about this and pursued the matter until he agreed to give a course of eight lectures on agriculture. One facet of the lectures had to do with compost. Steiner reasoned that forces brought into the compost pile carry on in the soil after the compost is applied. These forces are picked up by crops grown in that soil and, in turn, these forces are released into the livestock and the humans who consume these crops. These are spiritual forces, forces which produce good health, a certain sense of morality and the ability to cope with life's problems.

I think most of us realize, consciously or subconsciously, that we are children of the Earth. We are also children of the entire solar system. The solar system is a closely knit family of planets. Moon and the Sun. Far back in time all of these bodies had a common origin. We need the forces of all of these celestial bodies to make us "whole persons" in body as well as spirit. There are plants and animal organs which have a close affinity to these celestial bodies. By properly utilizing them we produce the Biodynamic preparations which channel these forces. These Biodynamic preparations go into our compost pile to which they channel the forces from their respective celestial bodies.

Since the compost pile is a representative of the solar system, I think it is fitting to make that pile in the form of a circle. Remember the wisdom of the ancient people and their intuitive use of different geometrical forms. Let's try to be at least as wise as they were. The Sun is in the center of our solar system, whereas the planets are on the periphery. We must try to conform to the model the solar system has set for us. The Sun (Preparation 504) goes in the center while the planets (Preparations 500, 502, 503, 506, 507, 508) go on the periphery. The Moon (Preparation 505) is somewhat of an anomaly since it goes in the center with the Sun (Preparation 504). Enlivened rock powders, much like the sunlight, are dispersed throughout the pile. I don't think the amount of rock powders dispersed throughout the compost pile is critical. If the pile is built in layers, probably several shovelfuls per layer would be fine. The pile should be oriented on a North-South axis even as the solar system is oriented within the zodiac. The Earth (Preparation 500) is placed in the north position.

What enlivened rock powder is indicated for use in the compost? Any of them would be good. Use the one you like the best or use the one most available. Lime promotes the formation of humates. Lime would be a good choice.

Farmers and large scale composters might find it difficult to make their piles in the form of a circle. They could windrow their piles in a North/South axis, BD 500 being in the north position and the other preparations placed as shown in the diagram.

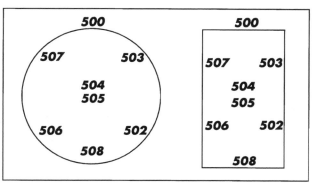

BD #	CELESTIAL BODIES	PLANT	ANIMAL PART
500	Earth	Cow	Cow Horn
501	Sun	None	Cow Horn
502	Venus	Yarrow	Male Deer Bladder
503	Mercury	Chamomile	Bovine Intestines
504	Sun	Stinging Nettle	None
505	Moon	Oak Bark	Skull
506	Jupiter	Dandelion	Bovine Mesentary
507	Mars	Valerian	None
508	Saturn	Equisetum	None

One set of compost preparations will treat any pile size up to ten tons. If the farmer estimates his pile at twenty five tons, he would need three sets. He would mentally divide his pile into three segments and install a set of the preparations in each segment. Holes can be made in the compost pile with a broom handle, the preparations dropped into these holes and covered up. BD 507, which is juice, should go into its own hole with no dilution or spraying. It takes from three to six months, depending upon many factors, for a raw compost to assume some humus qualities. The preparations are enzymes and are subject to heat deterioration if the temperature goes over 115°F. For this reason the pile should set for several days before the preparations can be safely inserted. The compost should not be turned, as this invariably causes a temperature rise and disturbs the formation of the forces.

There is nothing secret about how the preparations are made. Some of the methods are complex and time consuming so, especially for the beginners I would recommend that they purchase them from J.P. Institute, P.O. Box 133, Woolwine, Virginia 24185. Prices are modest.

In chapter 13, trees were discussed as a means for reestablishing or strengthening paramagnetic forces of the soil. Not mentioned was the option of painting the tree trunk with paramagnetic paste. The paramagnetic paste increases the paramagnetism of the tree to a marked degree, enabling the tree to become a more powerful factor in enlivening the soil.

The Biodynamic tree paste has a history dating back to the 1950s when Peter Escher developed it to promote tree health. It was originally formulated as a mixture of fresh cow manure and bentonite clay. Thinned sufficiently, it could be sprayed on the tree. It did not work out as a spray because of the difficulty in passing through the nozzles and wear on the nozzles.

In 1988 I took Peter Escher's formula and reformulated it several times, primarily to produce a tree paste with good paramagnetic properties. It was formulated as a paste to be brushed on the tree trunk to the height of several feet depending upon the age and size. Both the Biodynamic compost and the basalt have excellent paramagnetic properties, whereas raw linseed oil is the drying agent imparting resistance to the weather. Although I have used the basalt, any paramagnetic silica rock powder should perform well. The paramagnetic limes and clays would not impart the desired forces so should not be used. The compost must be screened to obtain a fine homogeneous material, easy to mix and easy to brush. Although the formula calls for the Biodynamic compost, which would work best because of its paramagnetic properties, any good quality compost could be used. The properties which I desired were:

1. Repelling or guarding against insect injury to the trunk from such insects as the peach tree borer, shot hole borers, etc.

2. Repel or guard against animal injury from mice, rabbits and deer.

3. Protection for incipient cracks in the bark occurring at trunk-limb junctions.

4. Should have some antibacterial and antifungal properties.

5. Should have some healing properties.

6. Prevent scald and winter injury to the bark.

7. Create a field of force which is beneficial to tree health and growth (paramagnetism).

The formula is:

Biodynamic compost, 2 cups

Basalt or any fine mesh paramagnetic silica rock powder should be satisfactory, 1 cup

Raw linseed oil , 3 tablespoons

Add water and mix well until a good brushable consistency is obtained. I use a Vita-Mix blender; any powerful blender will do a really good job.

I have been well pleased with its performance the several years I have used it. It may not have performed every function to perfection, but it has done well overall. I try to apply it once in the spring, once in the summer and once in the fall.

17

DOWSING

If you are interested in using paramagnetic rock powders in agriculture or nutrition or healing, or in any other way, then there must be some way of identifying that rock powder as being paramagnetic. Up to this point, dowsing has been the only method. Affordable instrumentation is not readily available now, but it is under development. Even so, many of us will still rely upon dowsing. Some may claim that a rock powder is paramagnetic, but it is much more satisfying to check it out yourself. Then, too, there are countless sources of rock powders which have not been classified. You may wish to make that classification, and if you are a dowser you can make that classification in a matter of seconds.

In my years of dowsing I have instructed many people in dowsing techniques. Well over 75% of the people I have instructed have picked up on dowsing. Some of the people caught on immediately. Others took a little longer, maybe up to half an hour. With this success rate I know dowsing comes naturally to most people and is easily learned. There are a few people who can't learn. I suspect that it is due to their mental attitude towards dowsing. If a person doesn't believe in dowsing and doesn't want to learn, then learning becomes impossible.

Dowsing is not scientific as we generally understand the term. It is an art or an intuitive response. To fall under the classification of a science, a subject has to be well under-

THE DOWSING ART

Dowsing is the art of detecting low-level energy. It is more art than science. *Intent* has a lot to do with it. Arthur Middleton Young, the inventor of the Bell Helicopter, held that one of the most amazing examples of animal behavior is the motion of an amoeba, which can reach out by extending a pseudopod, devoid of any musculature, from any place in the body. Chris Bird quoted Young as posing the question—*What causes the projection if it is not attention and intent?*

Like amoebas, dowsers project an intent to find, or a request for the location of a given object or target. What is projected? Perhaps a mental or psychic pseudopod of possibly infinite length. Whatever it is called, an answer to the request seems to be fed back via their bodies in the form of molecular movements which—because they are not consciously perceived—are called involuntary. The muscles cause the dowsing rod or pendulum to move, thereby objectifying the muscular action that, self-generated by the requester, cannot really be termed automatic.

Dr. Jan Merta, a Czech-born physiologist, psychologist, gifted psychic and professional deep sea diver worked on oil rigs in the North Sea. He was very interested in the water dowser's art as related to the extrasensory—map dowsing, for instance, location of lost children and successful searches for missing objects. Merta did a lot of experimental work at McGill University in Montreal. His findings caused him to suspect that the movement of the dowsing device had to be directly connected to muscular contraction in the body—specifically in the arms or hands. He therefore reasoned that if he could build an apparatus that could simultaneously record both the movement of the dowsing device and any muscular contraction, he would be able unambiguously to determine which came first, the contraction or movement of the device.

He electrically wired the *carpi radialis flexor* in the wrist area of the forearm. The instrument translated what was happening to ink and paper. After the several tests were finished, Merta concluded that the dowsing devices react only after human beings operating them pick up a signal which stimulates a physiological reaction. He further concluded that if the dowsing device were only an amplifier magnifying a sensation, then dowsers should be able to teach themselves to pick up such sensations without recourse to any dowsing device whatsoever.

He suggested that a projected request for information in dowsing is analogous to the number selection, the bodily reaction to the workings of the vast telephone switching system, and the final muscular twitching or neural response to the ring of an appropriate telephone on the other end of the line. In other words, a successful search depends chiefly on accurate formulation of the requests. Or, as the computer people have it, *garbage in, garbage out,* the recipe for failure.

—*Abstracted and extracted from* The Divining Hand, *by Chris Bird, and from* A Life in the Day of an Editor, *by Charles Walters* stood and findings must be repeatable, not only by the same person but by others. Dowsing is not well understood and the findings are not always repeatable. For the purpose of determining whether a rock powder is paramagnetic, dowsing works every time and is repeatable, and that is all we are interested in at the moment.

Dowsing can be used in many different ways. It seems to be limited only by the imagination of the dowser. The classical use for dowsing is the finding of water sources. Some people can use it to find lost objects, others to find lost children. As a race of people, the Chinese excel in dowsing. A Chinese family wouldn't think of building a house without first dowsing the building site for its suitability. Dowsing can be used to locate noxious forces which may be causing a disease problem or highway accidents. In this regard I could tell an interesting story.

U.S. Highway 250 runs near our property. In a period of five years, there were six truck accidents at exactly the same spot on the road. The road is straight and level with no intersections along that stretch. The accidents all occurred at night and involved trucks. Truck drivers notoriously drive too many hours and get overly tired. I am not being unfair to the truck driver with this accusation since I have a son-in-law who drives long hauls at night, and this is what he told to me. So an overly tired truck driver is driving along U.S. 250 late at night and passes over a noxious energy line. It affects him just enough so that he dozes off for several seconds and that is all it takes to run off the road. Within one week's time a truck had run off the road and crashed into a house. Another truck had run off the road at exactly the same spot and overturned in the front yard of the same house. The picture, of those two trucks, one in the side of a house and the other lying in the front yard, appeared in the local newspaper. When I saw that picture I told my wife that there had to be a noxious line crossing that highway. We drove down there and the trucks were still there. We made a mistake getting down there just as the kids were getting home from school. When the kids saw us walking along with dowsing rods in hand, their curiosity was aroused. They followed us to ask all kinds of questions. One mother came on the front porch yelling at us to keep off her yard. I yelled back at her telling her that we were on the highway right of way. As I had suspected, we found the noxious energy line about two hundred feet up the road from the spot where the trucks left the road. That was just enough distance for the trucks to meander off the road after their drivers had dozed off. I reported this to the highway department and they reacted exactly as I knew they would. The official courteously listened to me and dismissed the cause as not provable. The highway department did pacify the alarmed residents by resurfacing about one thousand feet of the road at that point. Later on my wife and I went down there one night when there would be no kids to bother us, and we neutralized the noxious line across the road. There have been no more accidents at that location. Did the highway department solve the problem, or did my wife and I solve the problem? Who knows?

I could go on with many other stories illustrating what can be done with dowsing, but we are primarily interested in dowsing rock powders for their paramagnetic forces. To get a better appreciation of the ability of a dowser to pick up forces, consider water dowsing. The classical approach to dowsing is dowsing for a water well. I can offer a rational reason why this can be done and succeeds most of the time. There are professional water dowsers who have a success rate of 95% and better—never quite 100%. What is happen-

LIFE FIELDS

At Yale University's medical school, an anatomist, Dr. Harold Saxton Burr, and a philosopher, Dr. F.S.C. Northrop, teamed up to elucidate how the celestial bodies could influence life. They put forward a new "electrodynamic theory of life," since confirmed by thousands of experiments, which indicated that every human being, animal, tree, plant, and microscopic organism possessed, and was controlled by, an electrical field. The "life field," as it came to be called, acted to repair, maintain, and renew cells that are the building blocks of all life forms and thus hold them in recognizable shape just as a magnet arranged iron filings sprinkled on a piece of paper into a consistent pattern. Measurable with great precision, life fields, reminiscent of "organo-electricity," were seen to vary around trees, in response to lunar phases, sunspots, and other astronomical evens. As Tromp suggested, this may be potentially important in determining what is taking place in the life fields of dowsers as they perform their work.

—*Chris Bird*
in The Divining Hand, *1979*

ing here? Water travels through the ground in gravel or sand veins because there is less resistance to its flow. As the water travels through the veins there is a certain amount of friction generated and friction generates an electrical force field. Nearly everyone has had the experience of walking across a thick carpet on a dry day and touching some metallic object. A spark flies and the person jumps. So the dowser walks along dowsing for water and he enters the electrical field created by the water flowing through the gravel vein. This is a force which comes through to the dowser as water.

Picking up the forces emanating from paramagnetic rock powders is the key to determining whether they are paramagnetic and not inert. Certainly, dowsing a rock powder is easier and simpler than dowsing for water. Either a rock powder has a force field or it doesn't. If it has a force field, the force field may spiral upwards in a counter-clockwise direction, indicating paramagnetism. Or it may spiral downwards in a clockwise direction, indicating diamagnetism. All the dowser has to determine is whether the force field extends upward or downward.

The easiest and most practical way to learn about dowsing is to get one-on-one instruction. The American Society of Dowsers, P.O. Box 24, Danville, Vermont, 05828, has three or four conferences every year. Each conference is preceded by a dowsers' school staffed with excellent dowsers. You don't have to be a member to attend. There are chapters in each state. If you have confidence that you could pick up dowsing on your own, and if you had a good manual, you probably could do this. Such manuals are available. Write for a book catalog from the American Society of Dowsers' Bookstore, 101 Railroad Street, Saint Johnsbury, Vermont, 05819.

I am not going to get into the actual techniques of dowsing since there are excellent manuals on this subject which go into more detail than I could here. I would like to say that dowsing is connected with the mind. Practicing dowsing sharpens the mind. I like to say that it is *mind power.* There are dowsable objects around everyone's home which can be used for practice. You can dowse the power lines or the water main coming into your home. They create force fields, therefore they can be dowsed. TV sets and microwave ovens give off powerful forces which can be easily picked up by dowsing.

The ancient peoples involved intuitive wisdom in building their megalithic structures—where to build, and how to use them. We have lost that wisdom, but we are now in the process of recovering it as intellectual wisdom. Certainly, dowsing is not the best method in recovering that wisdom, but it appears to be one of the best instruments we have at this time. Specifically, it can help us bring back the paramagnetism of the soils so valued by ancient peoples.

GRAMMAR OF THE SUBJECT

Rocks come under three general classifications.

IGNEOUS. These are the primal rocks originating from molten mixtures which over the space of many eons in time solidified. Many of our silica rock powders will be found originating in this group.

SEDIMENTARY. These rocks are extremely varied, differing widely in texture, color and composition. Nearly all are made of materials that have been moved from a place or origin to a new place of deposition. The distance moved may be a few feet or thousands of miles. Running water, wind, waves, currents, ice and gravity move materials on the surface of the earth by action that takes place only on or very near the surface.

METAMORPHIC. These are rocks which have been changed from their original. Changes may be barely visible, or may be so great that it is impossible to tell what the original rock once was.

With these few notes as a prelude, let's look at the grammar of the subject as set out in a few glossary terms. Those that follow are arranged alphabetically.

APATITE. A lime rock powder. While this phosphate mineral, $Ca_5(Cl,F)(PO_4)_3$, is not an igneous mineral, it is most often found associated with igneous minerals. It is crystalline in nature. An interesting fact is that bone has essentially an apatite composition and structure. To pursue this line of thought, our blood cells are born in our bone marrow, a location fraught with life forces.

AZOMITE. A proprietary montmorillonite clay, hydrated sodium calcium aluminosilicate, bearing many trace minerals. It has a volcanic origin. It is one of the few paramagnetic materials recognized as safe (GRAS) by the FDA. Clay.

BASALT. Another type of igneous rock which flowed out of the earth in the form of lava. It is also a member of the feldspar family and is high in silica. The Hoosac Mountain range of western Massachusetts has very large deposits of basalt. There are a number of quarries in the area from which basalt is easily obtained. A number of the New England farmers and gardeners are using this material. Silica.

BENTONITE. It comes from weathered volcanic ash and is noted for its high absorbency power. Clay.

CHILE SALTPETER. This product is better known as sodium nitrate. This substance is found in certain arid regions where it has apparently been formed by the decay of organic substances in the presence of air and sodium salts. The largest deposits are in Chile, and most of the natural nitrate of commerce comes from that country. Lime.

CLAY ROCK POWDERS. The clay fraction is the one which controls most of the important properties of a soil. Clays are the ages long breakdown of soil particles to smaller and smaller sizes. To be classified as a clay, the soil particles must be less than .002 mm in diameter. The clays are hydrated alumino-silicates with platelike structure showing marked cleavage. Their crystalline structure is determined by the spatial arrangement of oxygen atoms, which by weight constitute roughly half of the mineral content, although on a volume basis the clays are roughly 90% oxygen. The cation exchange capacity of a soil is determined by the clay and the organic matter. All clays are not paramagnetic. Location seems to govern the degree of paramagnetism.

CLOD BUSTER. A proprietary sedimentary material coming partially from the sea and partially from the mineral/plant kingdom. To quote its literature, it "is mined from specially selected strata of deposits remaining from prehistoric tropical rain forests and an inland sea. As the Earth's surface wrinkled and buckled, alternate layers of sea growth and dense forest growth were deposited. The organic matter failed to reach a sufficient concentration to form coal. It was reduced to humus and has been preserved in that state by overlaying layers of caprock." As is true in many other paramagnetic materials, Clod Buster has retained an element of life and has a significant silica content. Silica.

COAL. A fossilized mineral/plant material which would probably come under the classification of a metamorphic rock. Coal is mined as a fuel utilizing its carbonaceous component, but it also has a mineral component high in silica. In the very early days of Earth formation, before there was a plant kingdom as we know it, there was a mineral/plant kingdom to which coal belonged. It grew. It had life. Coal retains an element of life to which we can attribute some of its paramagnetism. All coal has paramagnetism. Silica.

DIATOMACEOUS EARTH. This probably could be classified as a sedimentary rock. It is a sediment. Millions of years ago, in sea waters, microscopic one-celled plants called diatoms, took the minerals from the water and created protective shells for themselves. They lived in great numbers and as they died their shells drifted to the bottom of the sea in great beds. Over eons of time some of these seabeds have raised above sea level and are now land areas. It is from these areas that diatomaceous earth is strip mined. Diatomaceous earth has a number of beneficial factors going for it, two of which we are especially interested in from a paramagnetic viewpoint. The shells are silica. It still retains an element of life. See the boxed material on page 45. Silica.

DOLOMITIC LIMESTONE. A lime rock powder. When magnesium carbonate is present in significant amounts, the limestone is designated as dolomitic. A typical dolomitic limestone will contain 40 to 45% magnesium carbonate and 50 to 55% calcium carbonate. Limestone as applied should be ground so at least 60% passes through a 100-mesh screen.

DYNA-MIN. A proprietary clay sold as a supplement for all classes of livestock. To quote its literature: "An active clay containing trace minerals in readily available form. Its micro-crystals are extremely fine grained and thin layered and are not tightly bound to one another so water, numerous elements and organic matter can enter the spaces between the layers." Although the material is a clay, according to my tests it has a paramagnetism characteristic of the silica rock powders. Silica.

FELDSPARS. These form the most abundant group of minerals. If the group were to be considered a single mineral, it would be the most common mineral by far. Feldspars are found in nearly all igneous rocks and in rocks formed from them. All are aluminum silicates combined with one or two more metals. Their crystal forms are very similar and the crystal angles are close to 60° and 120°. They usually have a smooth, glassy or pearly luster. Silica.

FLORA-STIM. A proprietary marcasite clay mined in Mississippi. It is usually high in iron and sulfur. It is used both in animal feeds and as a soil conditioner. Clay.

GRANITE DUST. Pulverized granite. It is being used by some organic and Biodynamic farmers in the area where it can be found.

GRANITE. A member of the feldspar family. It is the "stuff" out of which many mountain ranges have been formed. The Blue Ridge Mountains start in Virginia and extend down through North Carolina into Georgia. Just outside of Atlanta is Stone Mountain, which played an important role in the Civil War. It is a huge outcropping of almost pure granite. The granite in some sections pulverizes easily. Silica.

GREENSAND. Glauconite is an iron-potassium-silicate that imparts a green color to the minerals in which it occurs. The most common glauconite mineral is the greensand of New Jersey which was deposited near the "mud line" surrounding the continental shores many millions of years ago. As an oceanic deposit, glauconite is developed principally in the interior of shells. Organic matter is believed to play a part in its formation. Being an undersea deposit, greensand contains traces of many if not all the elements which occur in sea water. Clay.

GYPSUM. A lime rock powder that is generally a sedimentary

calcium sulfate rock occurring in massive beds. It is also known as plaster of paris from its early production from quarries in Paris, France. It is the constituent of the wall boards in most of our homes. "Lime."

HI-CAL LIMESTONE. The prince of lime rock powders. To be considered a Hi-Cal limestone, the calcium carbonate should comprise at least 90% of the total.

HUMATES. Humus or humic acid can be considered to be the same thing. It is well broken down organic matter. After being once broken down, the young humus starts polymerizing or building up into more complex compounds. Generally, the more this buildup process goes, the more valuable it will become to the soil. It may still be acid and not yet in its ultimate stage which is humate. It is helpful at this time to have some minerals to spread on the soil or to add to the compost pile which can combine with the humic acid to form the ultimate humate. The preferred minerals are calcium, magnesium, potassium or sodium. That is the prime reason for "liming" a soil or adding "lime" to the compost pile. For the most part, a young humic acid is paramagnetic. A finished compost is diamagnetic. Silica.

HYBROTITE. A type of granite dust found near Atlanta, Georgia. A number of years ago it was quarried commercially and mixed with specially composted chicken manure to produce Litter Life. Joe Francis was the developer of this product which, I can testify, was a very fine composted material. Silica.

HYDRATED LIME, OR SLAKED LIME. When quick lime is treated with water, hydrated lime results, $Ca(OH)_2$.

KAOLIN. Found extensively in the southeastern states since

it is a highly weathered type. Clay.

LANGBEINITE. A marine evaporite deposit of crude potassium sulfate, magnesium sulfate and sodium chloride. Most deposits in the United States are found in New Mexico. Lime.

LIME SLAG. In refining iron ore or scrap iron in an open hearth furnace, limestone is used to remove the impurities. After this molten material has been poured off and cooled down, it is known as slag. The slag contains the original limestone plus the impurities. It is a good product.

LIMESTONE. Obviously, a lime rock powder. Along with some impurities, limestone contains both calcium and magnesium carbonates.

MARCASITE. A common clay high in iron sulfide.

MARL. A lime rock powder that is a calcareous clay. Its genesis would be somewhat similar to that of rock phosphate. Marl generally contains significant amounts of iron sulfide and bituminous substances which account for the dark color. Lime.

MONTMORILLONITE. A type of clay distinguished by its capacity to absorb moisture at various humidities and by its relatively high silica content.

NUTRICARB. A proprietary coal derived from a bituminous coal blend high in sulfur. Silica.

PASCALITE. A proprietary bentonite clay mined in the Big Horn Mountains of Wyoming. It, too, has been recognized as safe (GRAS) by the FDA. It has found its best values in the healing area. Clay.

PERLITE. A type of feldspar which takes up water. When this water- permeated obsidian is heated, the rock swells up into a glassy froth. This expanded glassy material has many horticultural uses, one of which is as a medium for growing cutting and seedlings. It is not a clay but has the paramagnetism of a clay. Clay.

PHOSPHATE ROCK. A lime rock powder. Geologists commonly agree that phosphate rock was formed millions of years ago on the bottom of a vast sea which then covered a large part of what is now the United States. The phosphorous rich shells and skeletons of small marine animals settled to the bottom in a sedimentary deposit. These bones and shells hardened during the ages as the sea bottom rose to become part of the continent. Exposed to the elements this phosphatic limestone slowly weathered, began to crumble and break down. The calcium carbonate of the limestone dissolved in water and washed away in a natural refining process, leaving relatively pure deposits of phosphate rock.

PLANTERS TRACE MINERAL FERTILIZER. This also is known as *ELX Rock* Dust. It is a proprietary sedimentary material coming from the sea. To quote its literature: "An extraordinary combination of primordial events and environments was responsible for the formation and preservation of an exceptional mineral deposit located in central Colorado. During the geological past, vast inland seas occupied the interior of what is now the United States. Each withdrawal of these seas left deposits which were buried under sediments laid down by streams flowing off the recently exposed land." Besides its paramagnetic properties, it is also a good source of calcium and sulfur. Silica.

PRO-MIN. A lime rock powder that is a proprietary product rich in calcium, sulfur and trace minerals. It is partially soluble in water, which is an unusual characteristic of most rock powders.

QUICK LIME OR BURNT LIME. It is derived from limestone by driving off the carbon dioxide by high heat. It can be characterized as calcium oxide, CaO.

STACK LIME. The environmental age wants pure air unpolluted with sulfur. Since sulfur is the chief pollutant of coal fired power plants and the chief cause of acid rain, we must get rid of it. The sulfur can be removed by reacting it with lime as the combustion gases are given off from the furnaces. The resulting lime is now rich in sulfur. Rudolf Steiner has lots to say about sulfur and it is all to the good. Sulfur is one of the chief elements in three of the essential amino acids which make up proteins in foods. Soils should be rich, not only in phosphorous but in sulfur as well.

SYLVINITE. A marine evaporite deposit of crude potassium chloride and sodium chloride. It is found in the same areas as langbeinite. Although both langbeinite and sylvinite are potassium minerals, they come under the classification of "lime" as given by Rudolf Steiner. They are both diamagnetic and will perform the diamagnetic functions so important in soils and plants.

TACONITE. An iron ore from the iron range in Minnesota. It has the obvious advantage of an excellent iron source, but maybe of more importance is the fact that it has paramagnetic properties similar to clay. Clay.

TRAP ROCK. A name for basalt. It is the term used by the quarrymen. Silica.

VERMICULITE. A clay mineral containing water. When it is heated, steam forms and it explodes much like popcorn. It expands to many times its original volume. It is excellent for growing cuttings and seedlings. Clay.

ZEOLITE. See box on page 72. Of volcanic origin, zeolite has several family members, namely analcime, chabazite, heulandite, natrolite, and stilbite. All lose and replace water in their crystal structure. Analcime is isometric and hexoctahedral in its crystal formation, and the other family members have hexagonal, monoclinic, prismatic, etc. attached to their nomenclature. Clay.

INDEX

A Different Formula, 104
Abehsera, Michel, 2, 58, 70
Aborigines (Australia), 129
acid rain, 50
acid-alkaline, 81
Acres U.S.A., *xi*, 56, 68, 86, 89, 121, 123, 133, 135, 152, 153, 140
Acres U.S.A. Primer, An, 113
Acres U.S.A. Desk Reference, 67
additivity, 90
After the Ice Age, 83
Agri-Dynamics, 125
Agricultural Course, 5
Agricultural Lectures, 27
Agronics, Inc., 125
Alamosa, Colorado, 10
Albert Carter Savage, 66
Albrecht, William A., *x*, 9-11, 53, 54, 56, 63, 69, 87, 123, 124, 137
Albrecht Papers, Volume 1, 53, 54, 56
Albuquerque, New Mexico, 125
Alexander the Great, 134
Alexandria, Library of, 132
alfalfa, 12
alkaline-acid, 81
allegory, 26
alternative agriculture, 87
aluminum oxide, 1, 2
aluminum, 59, 61
American Institute of Dental Medicine, 10
American Potash Institute, 124
American Society of Dowsers, 145, 147
amethyst, 2
Amish farmers, 12
ancient wisdom, 129-148
Ancient Wisdom, 90

Ancient Mysteries, Modern Visions, 62, 133
ancients, knowledge of, 90
Anderson, Donald, 61
Anderson, Rollin, 127
Anderson, Arden, 69
animal kingdom, 22
Anthroposophical Society, 3
Anvil Mineral Products Company, 8
apatite, 49, 177
Arabs, 132
Asbill, Sandy, 154
Asians, 129
atom, 23, 24
atomic power, 158
Augustine, Saint, 144
auras, 107, 108
Austin, Texas, 71
Australia, 64, 107, 125, 127, 140, 155, 178

Bach, Edward, 115
Baja, Mexico, 85
basalt, 43, 47, 93, 95, 168, 178
Bay Springs, Mississippi, 8, 12, 61
BD 507, 164-166
BD 500, 164, 165
BD 501, 161
BD 506, 164, 165
BD 502, 164, 165
BD 504, 164, 165
BD 503, 164, 165
BD 508, 164, 165
BD preps, north-south axis, 165
Beach, Rex, 42
beam projector, 154
beast, the, 25
Becker, Robert, 157
bentonite, 58, 61, 178

Bergson, Henri, 31
Bertrand, Gabriel, 110
Bertrand's Law, 110
Better Crops with Plant food, 124
Bible, 1, 23-25
Bio-Dynamic Farming and Gardening, 105
Biodynamic agriculture, 7, 36, 160, 163
Biodynamic tree paste, 166
Biodynamic forces, 161-168
Biodynamic Farm, A, 160
biological farming, 87
biological transmutation, 94
Biological Theory of Ionization, 42
Biomin, 106
Bird, Chris, 106, 170, 171, 174
Birth of the Earth, The, 41
Blue Nile, 89
Body Electric, The, 157
boiling stones, 71
boron, 38
Boulder, Colorado, 155
Bread From Stones, 3, 117, 121
Brennan, Martin, 146
bromeliad, 38
Bromeliad Factor, The, 42
Bromfield, Louis, 87
Brookside Laboratory, *x*, 8
Burdick, Everette M., 98, 99
burnt lime, 185
Burr, Harold Saxton, 174

cabbage worm, 108
calcium oxide, 49
calcium carbonate, 49
calcium, 1, 8, 38, 50, 52, 69
Calcium Kingpin, The, 69
Callahan, Philip S., 34, 62, 89, 133, 136, 150, 152
Campe, Joanna, 123
carbon, 95
carbon 666 atom, 25
carbon dioxide, 59

carbon 666, 24
Carbon Connection, The, 48
carcinogen, class B, 157
Carlsbad, 55
carpi radialis flexor, 171
Case for Enlivened Rock Powders, A, 124
cathedral building, *xiii*
cation exchange capacity, 60, 75, 92
cell, the, 152, 153
Celtic people, 62
chalk, 35, 49
chemical agriculture, 84, 123
Cheops, pyramid of, *xiii*, 90, 132, 133
Chernobyl's fallout, 65
chestnut, 106
Chile saltpeter, 52
Chinese dowsing, 172
Chinese, 129
Christ, 1
chromatogram, 12
chromium, 2
circulatory system, 2
clay rock powders, 57-70
clay, 6, 7, 9, 12, 51
clay as rations, 2
clay's attraction, 58
Climate, diamagnetic forces, 108
Clod Buster, 36, 46, 93, 100, 102, 125, 140, 179
coal, 43, 44, 48, 52, 179
Coal Connection, A, 48
Cocannouer, Joseph, 87
cold, 97-108
Colorado Springs, Colorado, 125, 126
compost, 103, 146, 162, 166, 167
computers, 30
copper, 38
coral, 49
Corinthians 3:19, 24
cosmic bodies, 68, 70
cosmic forces, 161
cosmic Christ, 70
cosmic and earthly energies, *xiv*
Cosmopolitan, 42

Cosmos, 6
cow horns, 36
Creative Evolution, 31
Crick, Francis, 35
Cronstedt, Baron, 71
crystals, 29, 30
Cutler's earth, 2

d'Arsonval, Jacques Arsene, 152
Dallas, Texas, 17
Dana's Manual of Mineralogy, 72, 73
Danville, Vermont, 175
Dark Ages, *xiii*, 130
Davis, Albert Roy, 138, 145
de Chardin, Pierre Teilhard, 4, 31
Declining Soil Fertility, Its National and International Implications, 10
Delta, The, 89, 90, 91, 93
Democritis, 31
Development of Loessial Soils in Central United States as it Reflects Differences in Climate, The, 9
diamagnetic, 34, 52,
diamagnetism, 81, 146
diatomaceous earth, 34, 36, 44, 45, 93, 179
Diatomaceous Earth, 45
diatoms, 34, 44, 45
Dickerson, Ford, 61
digestion process, in plants, 55
digestion, 7
Dioscorides, 2
disease resistance, 97-108
Divining Hand, The, 171, 174
Dix, Byron E., 131
DNA, 35
dolomitic limestone, 180
Dowd, Michael, 4
dowsing, 85, 155-159, 169-176
Dowsing Art, The, 170
drought resistance, 101
drought, 97-108
dü Noüy, Lecomte, 26
dust of soils, viii

Dust Thou Art, 23
dusts of the soil, 1
Dyna-Min, 125, 180

$E = MC^2$, 17
Earth, birth of, 15-28
Earth energy, 157
Earth, 20-22, 24, 26, 27, 33-35, 41, 44, 46, 47, 52, 59, 79, 81, 84, 91, 97, 129, 130, 133, 138, 143, 146, 161, 164, 165
Earth energy lines, *xiii*
Easter Island statues, *xiii*
Easter Island, 136
Ecclesiastes, 3:14, 23
eco-farming, 87
Economic Botany, 99
Egypt, 132, 134
Egyptians, 129, 130, 135
Einstein, Albert, quote, ii
Einstein, Albert, 17, 137
electrodynamic theory of life, 174
electrolyte, 14
ELF Factor, The, 157
elm, 106
ELX Rock Dust, 184
Empty Foods, 42
energies, 29
energy, 17
Engelken, Rita and Ralph, 64
Enzyme Systems, 112
enzymes, 109-116
Escher, Peter, 167
etheric force, 139
Exploring the Spectrum, 150

Falb, Ike, 8, 12, 123
far planets, 27, 28, 78, 80
feldspar, 43, 96, 180
Fenzau, C. J., 69, 113
Fibonacci's series, 91
First National Conference on Land Classification, 9
Fletcher Sims' Compost, 119

flint, 39, 40
Flint Stones, The, 39
Flora-Stim, 12, 61, 93, 100, 123, 125, 181
Food and Drug Administration, 126
foods, empty, 42
Foreman, Jonathan, 87
Fram, Bob, 13
From the Soil Up, 139

Galileo, 31
Genesis 1:3, 23
Geo-Environment Service, 71
Geographical Review, 10
Gilgamesh, 2
glyphs, 135, 136
God, 17, 47
Grand Rapids, Michigan, 125
granite, 43, 47, 96, 181
granite dust, 181
GRAS, 126
Great Pyramid of Giza, 90, 132, 133
Greece, 132
Greeks, 132
Greeley, Iowa, 64
green thumb, 36
greensand, 64, 181
gypsum, 49, 50, 93

Hall, William Q., 45
Hamaker, John, 68, 123, 127
hard rock phosphate, 63, 64
hardpan, 12
Hardy and Killick, 133
Healing Through Ionization and the Equations of Life, 23
Healing Clay, The, 2, 58, 70
Heintz, Tim, 65
Hensel, Julius, 3, 117, 120-122
Hensel's Stone Meal, 121
Herschberger, Melvin, 102
hi-cal limestone, 182
high blood pressure, 2
High Aswan Dam, 89, 94
Hipparchus, 91

Holland, 104
homeopathic lime, 55
Hood, Samuel, 87
Howard, Albert, 87
human kingdom, 22
Human Destiny, 26
humates, 36, 92, 165, 182
Humates, 98
Huxley, Thomas Henry, 35
hybrotite, 182
hydrated lime, 182
hydrogen, 60

igneous rocks, 47, 177
Incas, 129
India, 132
Indians, 129
Industrial and Engineering Chemistry, 45
insect resistance, 97-108
intuitive wisdom, 130
Irish round towers, 136
iron, 1, 2, 8, 38, 59, 61

J. P. Institute, 166
Japanese beetles, 108
Johns, Dale, 155
Jupiter, 19, 20, 27, 28, 33, 41, 78, 161

Kaolin, 182, 183
Kaufmann, Klaus, 40
Kervran, Louis, 94
Keyserlingk, Count, 3
King Solomon's Temple, *xiii*
King's Chamber, 133
kingdoms, plant, animal and human, 22
Koberwitz, Germany, 3
Koepf, Herbert, 69
Kuck, Lucille, *x*
Kuck, E.R., *x,* 124

Lake Victoria, 89
Lakhovsky, Georges, 152, 153

Lancaster County, Pennsylvania, 12, 14
langbeinite, 52, 53, 183
Last Battle, The, 26
Lee, Royal, 87
Let Rocks Their Silence Break, 9-11
levity, 80
Lewis, C.S., 26
life, 32
Life in the Day of an Editor, A, 124, 171
Life Fields, 174
Life's Way, 83
light, 23, 41
lime, 6, 7, 28, 52, 69, 82, 93, 165
lime, burned, 50
lime, dolomite, 50
lime, feeding, 50
lime forces, 97
lime, high calcium, 50
lime, hydrated, 50
lime rock powders, 49-56, 156
lime slag, 183
lime, stack, 50
limestone, 135, 183
Lisle, Clarence, *x*
Lisle, Louise, *x*
living system, 33
Living Planet, 79
lodestone, 145
Lovel, Hugh, 160
Low Level Energy, 152
Lubke, Siegfried and Uta, 65, 75
Ludwig, Emil, 88
lungs, 2

Magnes Stone, The, 144
magnesium, 1, 38, 59
magnetic fields, 107, 108
magnetism, 61, 138
Magnetism, 144, 145
Magnetism and Its Effects on the Living System, 145
Mainline Farming for Century 21, 91
manganese, 1
Manitou, The Sacred Landscape of

New England's Native Civilization, 131
maple syrup, 81
maples, 106
marcasite clay, 8, 12, 123, 183
marl, 34, 183
Mars, 20, 22, 26-28, 33, 41, 78, 161
Martin, Robert T., 58
Martins Creek, Pennsylvania, 125
masons, *xiii*
material world, 3
matter, spiritual stage, 16
matter, stages of, 16
Mavor, James, W. Jr., 131
Mayan pyramids, 135
Mayan culture, 132
Mayans, 129, 130, 134, 136
McGill University, 170
megalithic man, *xiii*, 147
Mennonite farmers, 12
Mercator, 91
Mercury, 21, 22, 27, 28, 56, 78, 161
Merta, Jan, 170
Mesabi Range, 61
metamorphic rocks, 177
mica, 43, 96
Micro-Min, 8, 12, 14, 123
microlife, 13
microwave ovens, 156
mineral kingdom, 22
Mineralization, 67
Mineralization in Kentucky, 86
minerals, 109-116
montmorillonite clay, 125, 183
Moon, 20, 22, 28, 56, 57, 59, 60, 70, 136, 161, 164
mordenite, 75
More Food from Soil Science, 51, 56
Moses, 134
Mound Builders, 129
Mount Eaton, Ohio, 102
Murray, Maynard, 85
Myer, Clifford, *x*, 8, 13, 92, 123

N, P and K, 1, 117
Napoleon, 134
Narina tales, 26
National Agriculurual Limestone
 Association, 10
National Geographic, 20
Natural History, 2
near planets, 27, 28, 78, 80
Neptune, 16
nervous systems, 77, 78
New Waterford, Ohio, 125
New England stone mounds, 131
New Way of Thinking, A, 160
New Testament, 1, 23-25
New Zealand, 140
Newton, Isaac, 137
Newton, Sir Isaac, *xiii*
Nile River, 89, 94, 95
Nile Valley, 62
Nile, The, 88
Nitrogen, 116
Nichols, Joe, 87
Northern, Charles, 42, 69
Northrop, F. S. C., 174
noxious forces, neutralizing, 155-159
NutriCarb, 48, 93, 125, 183
*Nutrition via Soil Fertility According
 to the Climatic Pattern*, 10

obelisks, *xiii*, 136
On a Piece of Chalk, 35
opal, 2
organic agriculture, 163
organic farming, 87
Organic Farming and Gardening, 87
Organic Gardening, 141
organic matter, 13, 84
Organic Method Primer Update, The, 69
organic movement, 13
orgskin, 68
Origin of Species, 31
orthoclase, 43

paramagnetic, 34
paramagnetic clays, 12, 63, 70
Paramagnetic, Diamagnetic, 62
paramagnetic forces, 108
paramagnetic properties, 46, 47
paramagnetic rock powder, 64, 65
paramagnetism, 61, 71, 74, 75, 81,
 84, 85, 89, 100, 103, 106, 135-137,
 146, 155-157, 167
Pascal, Emile, 61
Pascalite, 61, 126, 183
peaches, 106
Peak Minerals, Inc., 107, 125-126
perlite, 61, 184
permaculture, 140
Persians, 132
Petrick, Vaclav, 68
Pfeifer, Ehrenfried, 87, 105
pH, 69
Phenomenon of Man, The, 31
Philosophical Connection, A, 31
phloem cells, 80
phosphate, rock, 49, 50, 184
phosphates, 63
phosphorus, 38
pi, 91
Piglou, E.C., 83
pineal gland, 2
pines, 106
plant kingdom, 22
Planters Soil Conditioner, 8, 13, 14,
 92, 93, 123, 125
Planters Trace Mineral Fertilizer, 184
Plato, 134
Pliny the Elder, 2
plowsale, 12
plum curculio, 108
Pluto, 16
polaric forces, 81
polarities, 21, 28
polarity, 34
potash, 12, 49
potassium, 1, 38, 52, 64
potato regions, 43

power lines, 156
prehistoric man, 137
primordial precursors, 52
Prince Caspian, 26
Pro-Min, 93, 185
Pyramid Energy: the Philosophy of God, the Science of Man, 133
pyramids, *xiii*, 133, 134, 135
pyro-electricity, 30
Pythagoras, 91, 134

quartz, 2, 37, 43, 96, 135
quick lime, 185

radiation, 158
radionics, 149-154
Radionics, 150
rainfall, 10
raised beds, 138
Rawls, Walter C. Jr., 138, 145
Reams, Carey, 42, 69
red oaks, 106
regenerative agriculture, 87
Reich, Wilhelm, 139
Remineralize the Earth, 123
Revelation 13:18, 24
rhythmical metal, 59-61
Ridzon, Leonard, 48
Ridzon Farms, 125
RNA, 35
rock phosphate, 93
rock powders, clay, 178
rocks, sedimentary, 177
rocks, metamorphic, 177
rocks, igneous, 177
Rodale, J. I., 87, 141
Romans, 132
Rome, 132
round towers, *xiii*, 136
rubies, 2

Saint Johnsbury, Vermont, 175
Salida, Colorado, 8
salt fertilizers, 81

saltpeter, Chile, 52, 178
salts in the soil, 105
sandstone, 43
sap circulation, 60
saphires, 2
Saturn, 16, 19, 27, 28, 33, 41, 78, 161
Savage, Albert Carter, 67, 68, 123
Schindele, Rudolf, 106, 127, 140
Schriefer, Donald, 139
Schroeder, Henry A., 110
science, 26
sea solids, 85
sea shells, 49
Secret of Life, The, 152, 153
Secrets of the Soil, 106, 127
Secrets of the Great Pyramids, 133
sedimentary rocks, 177
Semple, A.T., 69
Seneca Indians, 142
sheep, 140
silica, 6, 7, 8, 12, 28-30, 36, 37, 39, 40-44, 47, 49, 57, 60, 95, 97, 106, 107, 111, 123, 125, 126, 135, 138, 155, 157, 168
Silica, the Forgotten Nutrient, 40
silicon dioxide, 39, 40
Silicon Valley, 39
sitting locations, and directions, *xiii*
Skow, Dan, 91
slaked lime, 182
sodium, 38, 49, 52
soft rock phosphate, 63, 64
soil structure 97-108
Soil Complex, The, 51
Soil Fertility and Biotic Geography, 10
Soil, Grass and Cancer, viii
solar system, 19, 20, 26
Spanish moss, 38
Spencer, Herbert, 31
spiritual entities, 19, 22
spiritual world, 3
spiritual powers, 36
stack lime, 185
Steiner, Rudolf, *x*, 1- 8, 17, 15,

19, 21, 27, 36-38, 41, 43, 46, 50,
56, 57, 59, 68, 82, 87, 96, 107,
122, 138, 139, 143, 163, 164
steles, *xiii*, 135, 136
stone, enlivened, 33
stone circles, *xiii*, 136
stone mulching, 141, 142
Stone Family, 142
Stonehenge, *xiii*
Stone Mulching in the Garden, 141
Stonehenge, 148
Strite, Garnet and Larry, 100
Sudan, 89
sul-po-mag, 55
sulfur, 8, 38, 50, 52
sulfur dioxide, 50
Sun, 15-17, 20-22, 27, 33,
41, 43, 46, 56, 57, 59, 60, 70, 81,
97, 115, 133, 138, 143, 161, 164
sunshine, 109-116
Superconducting Supercollider, 17, 25
Survival of Civilization, The, 68, 127
sustainable agriculture, 87-96, 123
sylvinite, 52, 185

taconite, 61, 185
Taylor, Leland, 102, 140
The Universe, 4
throat, 2
Tiedjens, Victor, *x*, 51, 56
Tiger, Georgia, 154
titanium, 1
Tompkins, Peter, 106, 133
Trace Elements and Man, 110
Trace Nutrients, 110
Transeau's precipitation-
evaporation, 10
TransNational Agronomy, 125
trap rock, 186
tree, the, 80, 81
Trifoliae, 69
trigonometry, 91

Turks, 132
TV set, the, 155, 176

U.S. Highway 250, 172, 173
ultra violet rays, 43
Uranus, 16

Venus, 21, 22, 26-28, 56, 161
vermiculite, 61, 186
Vicieae, 69
vitamins, 109-116
Voisin, Andre, viii, 1, 25, 70
volcanic rock, 136
von Liebig, Justus, 3, 117-120
von Liebig's N-P-K Theory, 118
vortex patterns, 151

Walters, Ann, *xi*
Walters, Charles, *xi*, 11, 69, 91, 113,
119, 124, 171
warm stage, matter, 16
warmth, Sun, 27, 28
warmth, spiritual, 16
warmth, material, 27, 28
watermelons, 43
Watson, James, 35
weevil, alfalfa, 12
Weinberg, Eugene D., 110
Weinberg's Principle, 110
White Nile, 89
wisdom, 24
Woolwine, Virginia, 166
world periods, 135
World Ionization Institute, 23

Young, Arthur Middleton, 170

zeolite, 186
zeolite rock powders, 71-76
Zeolite Family, The, 72
zinc, 38